The Next-to-Final Solution

PETER LANG
New York · San Francisco · Bern
Frankfurt am Main · Paris · London

Joseph Fabry

The Next-to-Final Solution

A Belgian Detention Camp for Hitler Refugees

PETER LANG
New York · San Francisco · Bern
Frankfurt am Main · Paris · London

Library of Congress Cataloging-in-Publication Data

Fabry, Joseph B.
  The next-to-final solution : a Belgian
detention camp for Hitler refugees/ Joseph B.
Fabry.
     p. cm.
    Includes bibliographical references (p.   ).
    1. Refugees, Jewish—Belgium—Biography.
2. Fabry, Joseph B.   3. Jews—Austria—
Vienna—Biography.   4. Refugee camps—
Belgium.   5. Belgium—Ethnic relations.
6. Vienna (Austria)—Biography.   I. Title.
HV640.5.J4F33 1991 325'.21'089924—dc20
[B]   90-23285
ISBN 0-8204-1527-8   CIP

Cover design by Sue Lobel.

Printed in the United States of America.

Contents

My Fellow Refugees in the Camp................1

Preface...3

I.   Prelude in Prison 5

II.   A New Breed of Vagrants.................17

III. The First Revolt.............................27

IV. A Community of Rejects 35

V.   A Republic Behind Bars 45

VI. The Arrival of the Wolf Gang............53

VII. Women at Merxplas.........................63

VIII. Justice 1939....................................73

IX. The Price of a Sickroom...................87

X.   A Slap in the Face...........................99

XI. Three Letters................................111

XII. Merxplas Revisited.........................117

Postscript 121

References...123

Appendix...125

My Fellow Refugees in the Camp

(This book is dedicated to their memory)

Jakob Benedikt............................former Frankfurt attorney, now trustee of the internees

Richard Stein..............................former Vienna judge, now trainee in the cobbler class

Dr. Theodor Berman....................former head of Internal Medicine at the Vienna General Hospital, now "minister of health"

Ernst Holländer...........................former tax consultant in Vienna, now camp president

Erwin Neidhart.............................former union agitator in Berlin, now "propaganda minister"

Kurt Berber.................................former dancer at the Vienna State Opera, now nurse

Josef Klingenberg........................former professor of philosophy at Freiburg University, now "minister of education"

Herbert Waniek ....former clerk of the Danube Shipping Company, now in charge of the camp canteen

Fred Glogau................................former high school student in Vienna, now trainee in the cobbler class

Dr. Willy Kruger ....former physician in Vienna, now assistant to Bermann

Ludwig Sommer...........................former owner of a Vienna fashion salon, now teacher of the tailoring class

Koloman Gal...............................former trapez artist in Budapest, now farmer trainee

Peter Kraus ....former merchant , now trainee in the cobbler class

Otto Einhorn...............................former carpenter, now teacher of carpentry class

Max Hutt....................................former boxer in Vienna, now "minister of health"

Bernhard Klein ....former antique dealer in Vienna, now camp secretary

Siegfried Neumann.....................former comedian in Vienna, now barber trainee

Franz Jäger................................former bar pianist and street musician in Vienna, now "minister of entertainment"

Richard Berliner ....former actor and director in Berlin, now teacher of an English class

Heino Wolf.................................former gang leader in Vienna, now chief of camp police

Ignaz Minkus.............................former member of the Wolf gang, now teacher of the cobbler class

Salo Weinkraut...........................former member of the Wolf gang, now camp policeman

Hugo Jonatai ....former member of the Wolf gang, now camp policeman

Heinrich Lobositz........................former restauranteur in Vienna, now kitchen chief

Georg Kellner ....former vice-president of the Rothschild Bank in Frankfurt, now camp treasurer

Bruno Kostelka............................former barber in Innsbruck, now teacher of barber retraining

Paul Schramek.............................former hawker in Vienna, now camp postmaster

Heinz Mautner.............................former janitor in Vienna, now head of the cleaning crew

Peter Klamm ....former chemist in Linz, now teacher of the auto mechanics class

Hermi Schaub ....former cartoonist in Vienna, now teacher of the arts-and-crafts class

Robert Klimt.................................former pharmacist in Vienna, now assistant of Dr. Bermann

Rudi Jellinek ....former shoe repair man in Wels, now the first teacher of the cobbler class

Oskar Pitman ....former owner of a furrier store in Vienna, now teacher of the furrier class

Berthold Stern ....former bookkeeper in Vienna, now teacher of the piano-tuning class

Wives of Camp Inmates

Natascha ....wife of Jakob Benedikt

Karla..wife of Dr. Berman

Susi...wife of Willy Kruger

Berta..wife of Ernst Holländer

Lucille Clairmont.........................later wife of Koloman Gal

Belgians

Hubert Pleienberg ....an early Hitler refugee, now Belgian manufacturer and sponsor of the refugees at Merxplas

Helen Pleienberg..........................his wife, head of the Women's Auxiliary

Louis Pluvier.................................son of a Belgian member of parliament

Benno Siebenschein ....head of the refugee department at the Jewish Committee in Brussels

Cecilia de Vries............................head of the visa department at the Committee

André Vandenheuvel.................director of the camp at Merxplas

René Dierx ....main guard at Merxplas

Albert Lebret ....assistant guard at Merxplas.

Preface

I first described my experiences at Camp Merxplas immediately after I was released in 1939, the events still fresh in my mind. That early manuscript was a bitter condemnation of a world that could not find room for six hundred refugees from the Hitler terror. We had escaped to Belgium from the threat of what later became known as "final solution." The Belgian government interned us in a camp established for vagrants. There we were to wait until some country would grant us visas, but the world was tightly barricaded against immigrants. The manuscript was an account of what human beings are capable of doing to others. I titled the book *No Room for Six Hundred.*

Years later, when I became familiar with the existential philosophy of Viktor Frankl, himself a survivor of the holocaust, my focus shifted. What happened in that obscure camp on the Belgian-Dutch border needed to be recorded as an account of what human beings are capable of doing for themselves, even in desperate situations. I retitled the manuscript *The Merxplas Experiment,* and wished to present it as a footnote to the shameful history of the Hitler period, but more as a testimony to the glorious capacities of the human spirit.

Now, with millions of refugees and homeless in detention camps all over the world, the emphasis has shifted once more. For six million human beings, Hitler's "final solution" became a grisly reality. For hundreds of thousands the detention camps, of which Merxplas was one of many, often became transfer stations to the death chambers—"next-to-final solutions." I tried to find survivors of our Merxplas experiment. But only after this manuscript was at the publisher's was I able to find one (see Postscript). I should like to dedicate these personal recollections to the memory of the inmates of detention camps during the Hitler period and to those in present camps in hopes that the world will find a living solution for them.

Berkeley, October 1990   *Joseph Fabry*

I. Prelude in Prison

1.

In September 1938 Walt Disney's "Snow White and the Seven Dwarfs" showed in the biggest movie house in Brussels. I bought a ticket and went to see it.

I had arrived from Vienna the day before, with all my earthly possessions: a suitcase full of clothes, a portable typewriter, and ten German marks. The swastika-banded border control had made sure I exited with no more than the allowable amount.

I splurged one-tenth of it on Snow White. I felt insanely happy. I was able to walk on the streets without fear of being arrested. I did not have to scan passers-by for swastikas on their lapels. I could sit on park benches, a luxury not granted to Jews in Vienna. For two hours I lived in the world of Walt Disney where good triumphs and evil is punished.

There was no logical reason for my happiness. I had a doctor-of-law degree from the University of Vienna and was a published writer of short stories; but the laws I had studied were no longer valid even in my own country, and my ability as a writer was useless in non-German-speaking countries. I had no country, and no prospect of finding one to let me in. My past offered no support, my future only threats. I was like a man who has just come up for air in shark-infested waters. Happiness is the first breath of air.

The Jewish Refugee Committee in Brussels provided survival money for rent and food. We were 27 new arrivals that day. Dr. Siebenschein, a former attorney from Aachen, gave us forms to fill out and instructions of behavior: no loud German speaking, no large groups, no attention-getting. Most important: no job seeking.

Siebenschein was a role model: mousy, furtive, stooped as if constantly ready to glance over his shoulder to see if someone was looking.

Of the new arrivals, I was the only one with an entry visa. The others had crossed the border illegally, sneaking through woods, wading through rivers, following smugglers who had added humans to their contraband.

Through a device of my father, I was no refugee but a businessman. In one of the many desperate schemes Austrian Jews conceived to escape the death trap, my father bought a patent for me. It was a gadget installed in the overhead water tank of a flush toilet that regulated the water flow. I went from consul to consul in Vienna trying to convince each that granting me a visa would save his country water costs. No consul fell for such an obvious trick until a friend of mine persuaded a Brussels manufacturer to express interest. The Belgian consul in Vienna reluctantly granted me a one-month visa. The Nazis made me sign a paper that I would never return to Austria.

My visa was the subject of amazement and envy among my fellow refugees. Only Ludwig Sommer, a tailor from Vienna who had arrived two days earlier, was more envied. His cousin in Baltimore had sent him an affidavit, one of the preconditions for an American visa. An affidavit guaranteed that the immigrant would not become a public burden. Sommer still had to wait until his quota number came up. The United States permitted a quota of some six thousand Austrians to immigrate each year, plenty for normal times. But now tens of thousands of Jews took out quota numbers, even if they had no guarantor. I, too, had a number but no sponsor. I, too, envied Sommer. Not only did he have an affidavit but he was a tailor. The laws and language were different for Americans, but they needed pants.

Actually I was better off than many of my fellow refugees. Some of my short stories had been translated into English, and my friend and collaborator, Max Kühnel, had fled to England before the border was shut and sold one story to the *London Daily Herald*, with the prospect of selling more. The pay was phenomenal. From my share of one story I could live in Brussels, on a bare survival budget, for a month. I just had to lay low until the first check came in.

Every day swarms of new illegals arrived at the Jewish committee with tales of gloom and doom. Dr. Siebenschein's over-the-shoulder glances became more and more apprehensive: please, no conspicuous gatherings. We were asked to be nonpersons leading nonlives. We met in each other's attic rooms, sharing horror stories which happened to be true. In my own attic I typed out tales of love and lighthearted banter for which, I hoped, the *Daily Herald* would pay cash.

On October 9 my Belgian visa expired. Three days later a young policeman stopped me on the street and politely asked for identification. He looked at my passport. I explained to him, in my high school French, that the negotiations about my patent had lasted longer than expected, but my water saver would greatly benefit the Belgian economy. He nodded and handed back my passport. Then he gave me a form which he asked me to fill out and bring to the police station the next day.

My story stirred up a flurry of excitement at the Committee, where refugees met to gossip and warm themselves. We used the Committee like Viennese use their coffee houses. Others had heard similar stories. People were ordered to a police station and never heard of again.

"They ship them back to Germany."

"Oh no, they wouldn't do that. They know that means concentration camps."

"What do they care? Anti-Semitism doesn't stop at the border."

Opinions were divided between optimists and pessimists. "What are you going to do?" they asked me.

I was an optimist. I had a visa, though expired. I was not going into hiding, as the pessimists advised. My background made me believe in law and the world of Snow White. The evil stepmother may have poisoned the apple, but virtue always triumphs.

2.

The next morning a sergeant at the police station leafed through my passport with the big red "J" for "Jude" (Jew) and the expired visa. He took some time comparing me with my photograph. He had a small button nose and a massive walrus moustache, and spoke French so fast that I barely got the gist of what he said. It was something about formalities—photographs and fingerprinting. Then I was driven by a policeman through the streets of Brussels. We stopped at a fortress of a building and I was led through a gate that said in large letters: *Prison a Forest*. We entered a small room where a walrus-mustached officer behind his desk puffed on a fat cigar and squinted at me through the smoke.

"What am I doing here?" I asked and was aware that Professor Schläfrig, my French teacher, would have clapped his hands in mock desperation at the many mistakes I managed to make in these five words.

But the officer had understood me and he too uttered the magic word, "*formalité*."

As promised, photograph and fingerprints were taken. My pockets were emptied and their contents placed in a large envelope. To my repeated protests that there must be a mistake, the walrus answered benignly, "*Pas erreur,*" and handed me over to a chubby-faced guard. We walked through a steel gate, up a steel staircase, along a steel corridor flanked by steel cell doors. Every step echoed throughout the passageway. I didn't believe this was happening. This was Sing-Sing. I had seen the movie last year, about gangsters, murderers, and shootouts, and now here I was, a doctor of law, a writer of short stories, an author of cabaret skits. We stopped at steel door 366, chubby face produced a cluster of keys, the door clattered open, and I was in a cell, bare except for an iron cot, a wash stand, and a toilet. The door fell shut and I was gripped by the enormity of what was happening. This was not Snow White. It was Dreyfus.

I had seen the Dreyfus movie, too. I banged at the steel door, shouting, "I am innocent," as Dreyfus had done. I had a double vision of myself—standing there banging and screaming, and at the same time observing myself, as on the stage, a dramatic figure playing Dreyfus. The cell reverberated as my screams bounced off the cement walls. Finally, a small peephole opened in the door and an eye peered through, watery gray and impersonal.

"*Je suis innocent,*" I shouted.

The peephole closed. Exhausted, I dropped onto the cot. It was as quiet as the Vienna Woods at dusk. The stillness cuddled and comforted me. I felt drained and utterly forsaken.

Faint footsteps approached outside, getting louder. They stopped at my door and keys clanked. A tall, uniformed man, topped by a blue, cylindrical police hat, entered.

"*Je suis monsieur le directeur,*" he said.

'Ah', I thought. 'The mistake has been cleared up'.

I raised myself from the cot to greet him. He gestured to sit down again, as a host would to a guest. He sat down next to me, took off his high cap and placed it at his side on the mattress. A guard stood at the open door.

Monsieur le directeur began to speak in a slow, considerate manner, so I would be able to follow his French. I was not a criminal, he explained. The Belgian government was in a desperate situation. It did not know what to do with the swarm of refugees that came across the German border. He had no choice but to keep those who were picked up and sent to his prison. "*Mon coeur est brisé,*" he said. "I'm heartbroken." He lifted both arms, palms up, in a gesture of helplessness. "What can I do? We only have solitary cells, and I must follow prison rules. A formality." He implored me to understand. The guard would buy me anything I wanted from the prison canteen—cigarettes, chocolate bars, writing paper. The price would be subtracted out of the money taken from me. The *directeur* would send me books from the prison library. He would send me a barber. Things would straighten out.

It was useless to point out to him that I had a visa. It was expired. I had money to rent a room, would get more money from England, didn't have to work here. He looked downhearted. "You are no criminal," he repeated. "Hitler is the criminal. *La canaille!* "He shook my hand, picked up his hat, and left.

Ten minutes later the steel door clattered open again: the barber. He gave me the quickest shave and haircut I ever had, and kept chattering in Flemish, which I couldn't understand. Soon after, the guard handed me three well–thumbed books and asked what I wanted from the canteen. I ordered pencil and paper. He brought me a pencil, a notebook, and six pieces of stationery. The stationery was a sheet folded in two so there were four pages. The first page said in large letters, "*Prison a Forest.*" Why not "*à Forêt*" as I had learned in school? Probably Flemish. The page listed prison rules, printed in French and Flemish, about correspondence and visitors. The other three pages were lined as for school children.

The stationery presented a problem. I had been writing to my parents twice a week and they would worry if they didn't hear from me. They also would worry at a letter from prison.

I looked at the books. The first was about the song birds in West Flanders. The second told about the rites of passage of the Bantu in the Congo. The third was a book of prayers with the title, *Le Souverain de l'Universe,* the Ruler of the Universe.

The absurdity of the book titles helped. I momentarily regained my sense of humor and wrote to my parents. Don't let the stationery scare you, I wrote. It's just a formality. I am not treated as a criminal. The director just visited me. He sent me a barber, some books. I am here until the Belgian government straightens out my expired visa. I have peace and quiet to write new short stories for England. So I'll have money when I get out. Meanwhile I have free room and board.

While I wrote I began to believe what I said. Somewhere in the upper echelons of the Belgian government someone would decide what to do with us. Those with a visa, however limited, would get preferential treatment. The directives would trickle down to *monsieur le directeur*, and he would come to my cell and apologize. Meanwhile I was safe from the Gestapo, in cell 366, *Prison a Forest.*

3.

I took inventory of my temporary habitat. The cell was six by five paces with a cot in the center, a mattress, thin and hard, probably straw. One blanket, folded neatly, no sheet, one small hard pillow, probably straw, too. A wash stand with basin and water pitcher. A cake of soap smelling of disinfectant, pail and mop, a flush toilet with overhead water tank. The Belgian government could save thousands of francs if they installed my water saver in all their prisons.

Being a compulsive reader, I studied the rules posted on the wall. They were bilingual. A chance to brush up on my French and have a first lesson in Flemish. The rules listed 17 items that were forbidden, a code of behavior, and a daily schedule. Wake-up bell, 5 a.m., room cleanup 5:15, breakfast 5:30, exercise 9:00, noon meal 11:30, and so on.

My studies were interrupted by a shrill bell. I checked the rules. Right, 5:30 p.m.: feeding time in Zoo a Forest. Clatter on the corridor, becoming louder as the food cart approached cell 366. Doors creaked open and slammed shut. When mine was opened I was ready, as the rules decreed, with tin bowl, cup, and water pitcher. Three guards operated in unison. One ladled out soup from a tank on wheels, another splashed black coffee in my cup and slapped a slice of bread on top, the third filled my pitcher by dipping it into a barrel of water. The soup was pale with scraps of potatoes and threads of meat floating in it. The coffee was weak and lukewarm. This free room and board left something to be desired.

The rules on the wall told me to wash the dishes immediately after meals. Then they granted me free time. How do you spend free time in solitary confinement? I picked up *The Ruler of the Universe.* It described a good and just world. My world was shattered. As a guide to living, religion was as useful as Snow White. The happy ending was blocked by immigration barriers. The Snow Whites of the real world were chased and jailed and killed by the witches who were everywhere.

Neither a complainer nor an idler be, the book said in anti-quated French. Do not fritter away your precious hours, it advised. I tried to think up a short story the *Daily Herald* might buy, something about a young dashing lord and a pretty girl. But my mind was invaded by thoughts of my parents trapped in Vienna, worrying about their son, without a future, in prison.

A shrill bell interrupted my musings and the light went out. The ruler of *Prison a Forest* had decided to end the day at 8:30 p.m. I had no night clothes. I lay down on my cot and had another attack of rage.

4.

The next thing I knew was another shrieking bell. Clanging on the corridor. Breakfast. Black coffee and bread.

I felt strangely refreshed. There was something vital about the chemicals in my body at 5:00 a.m. which I never experienced. I sat down and scribbled in the lined prison notebook. My head was clear, and I could hardly write as fast as the ideas came. Lord Percy was only interested in sports and carousing. Of late also in Diane Witherspoon, whose father was president of the Shakespeare Scrap Metal Company. Father Witherspoon liked the idea of having a lord in his family, but insisted that Percy give up his frolicking ways and prove he had a business head. He sent Percy to Paris, to make a deal with Monsieur Labouche, president of Molière Metals. Percy was to negotiate a contract favorable to the interests of his future father-in-law. Percy, however, fell in love with Michelle Labouche, daughter of the metal king, and to prove his love signed a contract ridiculously advantageous to Father Labouche. Punchline: he did what he set out to do—favoring his future father-in-law.

I had barely gotten Percy to Paris and his first fatal glimpse of lovely Michelle when the bell announced time for morning exercise. I was let out onto the steel corridor. From the rows of doors crept gray figures. We shuffled along the corridor, ten feet apart, single file. On the wall next to the gate that opened into the courtyard flickered a gas flame. As the inmates passed by, they fought for a place to light a cigarette. The rules in my cell specified that we could buy cigarettes but smoke only during exercise break. I did not smoke and had paid no attention. In my short stories, smoking cigarettes was a mark of sophistication. I now saw it as raw, brutal, ravenous craving. It turned humans into jittery animals.

The yard was large, with shaggy patches of grass, surrounded on all sides by cement walls that stared at us with hundreds of barred windows. To the blare of piped-in music we marched briskly and silently in a large circle, ten feet apart. Rule number 14: no talking.

All except six wore prison garb. The six wore suits like myself. This was the only distinction between thieves, robbers, and murderers, and the victims of thieves, robbers, and murderers.

I recognized one man in the circle. We had talked at the Refugee Committee. He attracted my attention because he had the same name as my maternal grandfather, Jakob Benedikt. He was an attorney from Frankfurt, tall, wiry, with tousled hair that looked at the same time elegant and slightly disheveled. When he wanted to make a point, which he did frequently, his intense charcoal eyes widened and flashed. He was married to Natascha, a flaxen-haired beauty with a childlike voice in a body that was all woman. She had fled from Russia as a child, after the revolution.

"It's my second time around," she had chirped. "I'm a double refugee."

Benedikt, smoking, seemed purposely to keep out of step with the march music. He was sauntering nonchalantly, for which I admired him. Another suit wearer was gray haired, balding, heavy rump on spindly legs, eagerly but vainly trying to keep up with the prison-garbed gorilla in front of him. One of the refugees was a boy, probably still in his teens, looking scared. Behind him walked a slim man with fine features and gold-rimmed glasses which he kept adjusting nervously. He wore a black turtle-neck sweater that made him look like a priest. On the opposite side of the circle were two more refugees: a frail, red-headed man, hunched over, furiously chain-smoking, and a scholarly looking professor, with a limp that made it difficult to march briskly. From time to time a guard stepped up to spur him on.

I speculated how we six had been selected out of the hundreds of refugees in Brussels. Old, young, married, single, even "legal" immigrants like myself. I counted 83 in the circle. Was our not wearing prison garb to mean we would be released soon? How long can you be without a change of clothes? The rules posted in my cell said something about a shower twice a week. I had to ask the guard to buy me a tooth brush. Did the prison canteen sell underwear?

I became aware that Benedikt was trying to get my attention. Whenever we rounded a curve he looked at me and pointed at his cigarette. Did he need money? I rubbed the tips of thumb and forefinger together, a sign language in Vienna for "money." He understood and smiled "no." He pointed to his mouth and moved his lips. I shrugged, indicating that I didn't understand. He smiled again, and when we passed the gate he pointed at it. For the next few rounds I puzzled over his possible message.

Another bell ended exercise time. We were marched back to our cells. When Benedikt turned into his and I walked by, he again looked at me and moved his lips. Back in my cubicle, I scribbled in my notebook. School is no preparation for life. It's a preparation for prison: no talking, rules for everything, time regulated by a bell, an hourly time table—not Latin and math, but washing floors and exercising. The books you read are boring, you can't go home when you want, and you're released with a final report card.

Time crept along slowly. I tried to think about my short story, but the chemicals in my brain didn't work. I was actually waiting for the next bell. In the afternoon I thought up a game: what would members of my family do in this situation? My father would hook his pince-nez onto the bridge of his nose and write down a list of ways to get out here. I couldn't think of any, but he would. My mother would worry about father and keep busy with pail and mop. She would count the bars on the window to see if they added up to thirteen, which would be a bad omen. I counted them, they added up to twelve. Bad enough. It was difficult to visualize Grandma Ida with her grand-dame demeanor. She would keep calling for *monsieur le directeur,* to complain. She would expect him to kiss her hand. I hated to kiss her wrinkly hand. Uncle Hugo would arrange an international chess tourna-ment, using illustrations from *The Birds of West Flanders* for chessmen. Cousin Elsa would spend hours blaming herself, trying to figure out what she should have done differently. Uncle Camill, a man in his forties but a boy at heart, would make a ball out of paper and play soccer solitaire against the wall.

5.

At five the next morning my creative juices flowed again and I finished my story before exercise time. While the smokers crowded around the flame I caught Benedikt's eye. He winked me closer, and I understood yesterday's message. He wanted to talk to me, and the cigarette lighting offered our only chance. I braved the stampede and maneuvred myself next to him.

"They're sending us back to Germany," he whispered.

I stared at him, unbelieving.

"Natascha told me. She visited me yesterday. You must tell them a hardship story. Being Jewish isn't enough."

That was all the time we had. The guards herded us through the gate into the yard. I looked around the circle. Ten suit wearers, but the mousy chain smoker and the limping professor were missing. Was the rumor true? Were two shipped back and six others readied for shipment? I walked in a daze, trying to think of other reasons why the two were missing.

Back in my cell, I asked to see the director. He was out of town, the guard said. Could I see someone else? After a long wait a young man entered, blond, blue-eyed, with a little blond brush under his nose. A bad omen. Instead of the sympathetic *directeur,* they sent this Hitler type.

I asked about their plans. He shrugged. I told him about my visa, my patent, my expected money from the *Daily Herald.* He didn't believe a word. I became exasperated. My brain short-circuited.

"Listen," I shouted. "I need underwear."

He looked startled, even a bit afraid. "I'm not a criminal," I continued.

"I don't get prison garb. How do you expect me to wear the same clothes, day and night, for weeks?"

"It won't be weeks," he said.

I was on a one-track path. "I need pajamas, socks, underwear."

It made me feel good to see his cocksure arrogance dissolve. Clearly, he had never faced this problem before. He pointed to the posted rules and said something about visitation rights.

"I've read this," I told him. "I have no spouse, no close relatives."

"In your case," he grinned, "the rules can be relaxed. Any friend can bring you underpants."

His irony made me furious. "I have no friends in this whole wide world," I bellowed.

"How about your important business connections?"

He had seen through my hoax, and this made me even angrier. "Listen," I said. "the man in 358 has a wife. My address and my room keys are among the things you people took from me. Ask her please to bring me a change of clothes. And my toothpaste."

"Sure," he said, retreating toward the door. "I'll talk to 358."

I was alone. The bubble of victory burst. I had acted like an idiot. Instead of a permit to stay in Belgium I would, perhaps, get a pair of underwear. I had antagonized the blond Hitler. I would be the first to be shipped off. "It won't be weeks," he had said. That could mean release or deportation. All of a sudden my prolonged stay at Prison a Forest did not seem so insufferable, even without a change of clothes.

Tell them a hardship story, Benedikt had advised. I did not have to invent one. I had been editor of *Die Muskete,* a satirical weekly that ridiculed the Nazis. Being shipped back meant concentration camp for sure.

As the afternoon dragged on, my spirits revived. It was inconceivable that I would be sent back to certain death. I lay down and fantasized a dialogue with the police chief. I cleverly countered all his arguments for returning me to Vienna. I tried to twist the dialogue into a short story with appeal to British readers. It didn't work. British readers weren't interested in Austrian refugees. They wanted to read about whimsical banter between a London bobby and a thief he'd caught. But nothing would come. My mind was at low tide.

I dreamed about the blond guard accusing me of stealing a suitcase full of jewelry. When he opened it, he found nothing but dirty underwear. At 5 a.m., after the black morning fluid, the pieces fell into place. My story was about Jimmy who stole an elegant suitcase in a hotel lobby and was caught by a policeman. Jimmy insisted the suitcase was his. When the policeman opened it, he pulled out yards and yards of colored streamers, a huge bouquet of flowers, two rabbits, and a giant British flag. It was the suitcase of a magician.

6.

At exercise, the number of refugees had increased to fifteen, but six of the old ones were gone. Deported? I had no chance to get close to Benedikt. He looked downhearted.

Back in my cell I felt utterly forsaken. Then I noticed that I wasn't alone. A column of ants marched down the wall from the barred window, across the wash stand, to a place near the door. I had seen one or two ants before, but now they had discovered a crum of bread, and the word had spread. They marched, mindlessly, not the shortest route but the path their *führer* led. My frustration vented itself, and I pounced at the orderly column, stamping to death as many ants as I could squash. The floor was strewn with corpses, and survivors scurried in all directions. I went after them, smashing them with passion, singly and in clusters.

Surprisingly, some survived—in cracks of the floor, in the protection of an unevenness, or without any apparent reason. A few emerged from under my shoe where they were sheltered by some tiny dimple in my sole. Some, seemingly dead, struggled back to life and limped off on their remaining four or five legs.

I sat down on my cot. Was this how the Ruler of the Universe operated? Was our life dependent on whims and flukes, on being sheltered in the random cracks of our existence? On being saved in a dip in the sole of the Ruler? A deep despair overcame me that lasted the rest of the day.

The next morning, at the cigarette flame, I managed a brief moment with Benedikt. "Pleienberg can help," he whispered before we were separated by the rampaging smokers. I had no idea who Pleienberg was but drew comfort from the knowledge that there was *someone* who could help. The number of suit wearers was ominously reduced by five, including the scared youngster. There were no new refugees in the exercise circle. Encouraging.

This straw of hope was crushed the next morning when 15 newcomers appeared. On the other hand, none of the old ones were missing. I spent hours speculating on possible scenarios. Did Pleienberg help?

If so, how?

The guard brought me a letter from Max. He was alarmed by my arrest. The news from London was good. The *Daily Herald* had bought another story but the first one was still unpublished. Max included three pound notes, his advance of my share. The letter had been opened by the prison censors and the money was being held.

My chemicals started to bubble again. Surely, they wouldn't ship a man to certain death who sold stories in England and got paid in British currency? Max's letter inspired me to scribble a story in my notebook about a man in London who fell in love with a girl in Glasgow. They wrote each other every day. For three months their letters crossed in the mail daily, but then the tone of hers cooled strikingly. He was puzzled until he got one last note from her. She had married the mailman.

The number of refugees in the exercise circle rose alarmingly, and some of the old ones dropped out. In my brief moments with Benedikt we exchanged guesses. I sat on my cot for hours listening at every footstep. It was as bad as in Vienna when we listened at night for the Gestapo to pick us up.

Familiar footsteps were not threatening—leading to meals, exercise, showers, and the twice-a-day routine inspection. Unexpected footsteps made my heart do somersaults.

On the sixth day unscheduled footsteps stopped at my door, and it clanked open. Every muscle in my body tensed. The nails of my clenched fingers dug into my palm. The guard entered and handed me a paper bag.

"From 358," he said.

The bag contained pajamas, socks, and underwear. This was not just a set of clothes, it was a message of hope. They would not send me pajamas if they intended to ship me back to Germany. Or would they? Common events became ominous—the expression on a guard's face, a large piece of meat in the daily soup (the last meal?), a new visit of the barber, the waxing and waning of suit wearers in the exercise circle.

On the ninth day, my heart jumped to my throat. Benedikt was missing. Although we had exchanged only a few whispers he had become my anchor. I was certain to be next.

7.

I spent all day and most of the sleepless night arguing with my imaginary judge and executioner. The ants swarmed all over the floor despite my frequent attacks. Some survived, some didn't. If they could talk, what would they say to convince me to let them live?

The next morning, halfway between breakfast and exercise, sinister footsteps stopped at my door. The guard entered.

"Take your things and come with me," he ordered.

"Where are we going?"

"*Monsieur le directeur* wants to see you." His face was a mask of indifference.

Following him numbly on the nightmare steel corridor, I tried to recapture my arguments, but my mind was empty.

The director again played his role as the superpolite host. He rose from behind his desk and gestured me into a chair.

"*Je suis désolé,*" he said, and my throat contracted at this expression of regret. But it turned out that his regret was merely about his failure not to have visited me again. Important business trips, he said.

His cheerful face brightened even more. "In fact," he continued, "the trips were about you."

The 'you', it turned out, was not me personally but all illegals that posed such a headache to the Belgian government. The Bishop of Liège had intervened to find a humanitarian solution. All technicalities were sorted out, and I was to be released into the custody of the Jewish Refugee Committee who would arrange our transfer to the camp of Merxplas.

"A camp?" The word sounded ominous.

"A beautiful *établissement. Une colonie de bienfaisance.*"

When I looked puzzled he went to the book case and handed me a dictionary. *Colonie de bienfaisance* translated as 'settlement of charity'.

"Everything will be all right," he assured me. "I am very happy for you."

"How long will we stay there?"

"Only until a permanent solution is found. Don't worry. Monsieur Pleienberg will explain the details."

We shook hands and he turned me over to a guard who handed me the paper bag with the things they had taken from me. He also presented me with a *Certificate de Mise en Liberté*. The graduation report card from *Prison a Forest*.

A police car took me to the Refugee Committee. I joined a small group of men in the waiting room. To my delight, Benedikt was among them, and so was the scared youth who had been missing in the exercise circle.

All were graduates from various prisons and all had heard various and conflicting rumors. The longer we talked, the more confused we became. Then the door opened, and Ludwig Sommer entered with the self-assured stride of a man who not only has an American affidavit, but a globally useful trade. He was able to separate facts from rumors.

The plan was contrived by Hubert Pleienberg, an early Hitler emigrant who in 1933 could still bring his money to Belgium. He now was a leading manufacturer of water pumps. His motive to "help" refugees (and Sommer pronounced the word in heavy quotation marks) were twofold: to move new arrivals out of sight before they aroused resentment against all refugees, including early ones like Pleienberg; and to "help" (quotation marks again) the Belgian government with its tricky refugee problem. Pleienberg had political ambitions.

What about this camp at Merxplas?

Sommer knew about that, too. "A labor camp for vagrants. The police picks them off the streets. In the camp they are forced to earn money, making straw brooms, and such."

"I don't believe it." A distinguished massive man spoke in a no-nonsense tone of voice. He had been a judge in Vienna and stared at Sommer with steely gray eyes under shaggy eyebrows, as he might have stared at a discreditable witness.

Sommer was offended. "Sommer knows what he's talking about," he pouted.

"Then why do you go to a reform house," the judge cross-examined. "You, with your American visa?"

"That's exactly why," Sommer said. "My quota number will be up in a few weeks, and meanwhile I'm safe." He looked over his shoulder and explained in a low voice, "They've been shipping back a dozen or so every day."

"I don't believe it," the judge decided again.

"Sommer knows what he's talking about," Benedikt said quickly before Sommer could say it himself.

8.

The door flew open. The man who entered was plump, his baby face camouflaged by a pair of horn-rimmed glasses and a mustache. He wore elevated shoes and a striped suit with padded shoulders and lapels wide as angels' wings. His crimson tie matched the handkerchief peeking from his breast pocket. Hubert Pleienberg.

It turned out that Sommer really knew what he was talking about. The Belgian government was in a predicament, Pleienberg explained in a squeaky voice he tried to bring down to baritone. Unemployment was high, food and housing in short supply, and hundreds of penniless refugees were swarming across the border. The Belgians still remembered the atrocities the Germans committed in the last war. Most Belgians did not distinguish Germans and German-speaking refugees.

"In Germany they hate us as Jews. Here they hate us as Germans," said the priest look-alike with the turtleneck sweater whom I knew from the prison courtyard. He said it as statement, not as accusation.

"That's the way it is," Pleienberg said. "The government started with arrests and deportations. We had to do something, and fast. I contacted the Ministry of Justice, and after long negotiations I was able…"

No mention of the Bishop of Liège. It was Pleienberg all the way. *He* had established the refugee committee. *He* had raised money for the weekly allowances. *He* had delayed the arrests. And now *he* had found the solution to prevent deportations.

"What is Merxplas?" Benedikt asked.

"A fabulous experiment in social rehabilitation. Experts from all over the world come here to study it."

"A camp for vagrants?" the judge asked bluntly.

"People with insufficient means are given a chance to become self-supporting citizens. They grow their own food, cook their meals, learn skills. When they are judged rehabilitated, they are returned to society."

"A camp for vagrants," the turtleneck said gently.

"You have nothing to do with the other subjects in the camp," Pleienberg explained. "The government has set aside two large dormatories and other facilities, completely separate, directly responsible to the camp director."

"A prison," the turtleneck said, adjusting his glasses and smiling shyly.

Pleienberg looked at us with determined, hard-as-steel eyes. "Listen." His voice again became high-pitched and splintery. "It's either Merxplas or Germany. I did what I could. Now it's your choice." He forced his voice down an octave. "You have your discharge papers from prison. That legalizes your stay in Belgium until Monday. That morning, at eight, the first contingent will leave for Merxplas. You are that contingent. The pioneers, if you will. It buys you security. Those of you who will not be here Monday morning"—he shrugged —"I cannot guarantee anything."

This gave us three days to make that decision.

"What about our wives?" Benedikt asked.

Pleienberg hid behind clipped factuality. "The camp is for males only. Wives will have to stay in Brussels. As long as you are in Merxplas, the government will take no action against them."

Perplexed silence. Benedikt paled. "How long will we stay at Merxplas?"

"I have established a special section at the Committee to secure oversea visas," Pleienberg said. "I'll see to it that they'll go first to you folks at Merxplas." He plucked out his crimson kerchief and dabbed his forehead. " I did the best I could under the circumstances. The best anyone could do. The camp is in the famous heath area at the Dutch border. I'll go with you myself Monday morning, to see that everything is all right. See you then."

He turned on his elevated heels and left quickly. Dr. Siebenschein stuck in his worried head. "Come and get your weekly allowance. And, please, no loud German-speaking in the streets."

A blond giant in a leather jacket and tight-fitting breeches, who had kept himself aloof, grinned, revealing two gold front teeth. I had wondered about him, he wasn't like the rest of us. He looked like a sailor: a robust figure with calloused palms and a face as if whacked out of a wood block by a primitive artist.

"For the next three days," he boomed out in unadulterated Berlinese, "I can speak as much and as loud as I want." He slapped his weather-beaten jacket. "I've got my pass from the clink."

II. A New Breed of Vagrants

1.

Monday, October 24, 1938. When I recall the day now, I see a little heap of human desperation huddled in a half-empty railway coach rattling through the flat Belgian landscape. As I reread my manuscript, written in German half a century ago, the shadowy figures I described emerge from the haze.

I don't remember their names, because I changed them. This was a symptom of the time: we were scared to name names and tell facts. When my parents wrote that cousin E. had gone on vacation, I understood that cousin Elsa had been taken to a concentration camp. A schoolmate whose name was Fritz signed his letter "Franz" and told me that our mutual friend, Heinz, moved in with his sister. I understood that Heinz was dead because his sister was buried in the Vienna Central Cemetery. It was a time when we learned that the truth shall make us prisoners.

Of the people on the train, the only real name I know for certain was Jakob Benedikt, my grandfather's namesake. He sat alone, hunched over, deflated, hands dangling between his knees. I had watched him say good-bye to a prim and ostentatiously cheerful Natascha. I knew three of the other men from the prison yard. In the 1939 manuscript I had named them Herbert Waniek, Ernst Holländer, and Fred Glogau.

Waniek wore the same turtle-neck sweater and expression of resignation he had worn in prison. He stared emptily through his gold-rimmed glasses the curved lenses magnifying his raisin eyes. From time to time he ran his tongue over his lips. I later learned that he was what he self-deprecatingly called a "paper shuffler" at the Municipal Danube Shipping Company of Vienna. This had been a well-known breeding ground for bureaucrats. Waniek distinguished himself from the prototype bureaurocrats through his special brand of irony.

Holländer was the chain smoker with a horseshoe of red hair raked across his freckled bald dome. He was a thin man with a thin face and thin hands, and a meek voice which we heard first on the train when he jumped up, bowing furiously, to offer Pleienberg his window seat. Holländer had been a tax consultant in Vienna, and I knew the type from my short stint as an attorney's assistant. The Austrian tax system worked like this: the tax payer declared about half of what he earned because he knew that the revenue officer who checked his return would assess twice the amount declared. If things got sticky, the tax payer hired a consultant who went to the revenue officer and, with much scraping and bowing, wheedled the tax down to an amount acceptable to both. Since Jews were excluded from government positions, many became private consultants and fawned before the "Aryan" and usually anti-Semitic officials. Holländer was type-cast for the part.

Fred Glogau looked like a high school kid and, as I found out, that's what he was. He stared at us with utterly confused eyes. He and Holländer had actually been shipped back to Germany, handcuffed and guarded. They were let out in Aachen, the first German stop beyond the border. The Nazis were not yet aware of this new Belgian policy of returning human merchandise and did not immediately arrest them. Holländer went to the smuggler who had helped him a few weeks before and, for the price of a gold watch, again sneaked him across the border. Glogau, having no valuables, made it on his own at night through the forests.

Glogau had good reason for trying not to get caught again. He was in the kind of trouble with the police typical of Austria in the year One of the Thousand Year brown empire. He had been walking with his father through the streets of Vienna when two brownshirts jumped his father, beat him up, and snatched a radio he carried. Fred defended his father and grabbed back the radio. A policeman walked by, and Fred turned to him for help. The policeman arrested Fred. He spent three weeks in jail and was released after signing a promise to leave Austria within eight days. His parents were happy to see him back from prison. "Lucky they didn't ship you to a concentration camp," his mother said. This was a time when the saying became common among Viennese Jews: "God save us from all things that are 'lucky'."

Glogau sat on the bench in our wagon, crying silently. Tears hung on his long lashes and trickled down the side of his freckled nose. From time to time he wiped them off with the back of his hand, never taking his cornflower-blue eyes away from the inner images only he could see. After a while, the bulky man with the feline head and the caterpillar brows, whom everybody called "the judge," moved beside Fred and talked softly to him. I couldn't hear what he said, but both expressions changed, Fred's from wan to boyish, the judge's from downcast to avuncular.

The judge, named Richard Stein in my manuscript, and Benedikt became my closest friends in the camp. We three had law degrees, and Stein always addressed us as "Herr Kollege." To be a judge in Vienna he had to convert to Christianity. This was a customary formality for Jews who wanted to make a career in government but conversion, which had saved Jews even during Inquisition, did not work under Hitler. You could not baptize away your "race." Hitler did not so much object to Moses as to your grandmother.

Judge Stein's additional misfortune was that he had sentenced a murderer to ten years in prison. The man turned out to be a Gestapo official who now became the judge of the "new" criminals, including those who had sent Gestapo murderers to prison. Judge Stein was "lucky" to escape.

Stein was married to an "Aryan" woman and had a son about Fred Glogau's age. What I saw on the train was the beginning of a close relationship which gave both men what they missed. Before the year was over, their bond would end in tragedy.

2.

Know-all Sommer also was with us, and so was the gold-toothed Berliner who didn't fit into our grim-faced group. He was a blocky figure, his solid jaw was crossed by a scar, and he darted quizzical and, it seemed to me, mocking glances at us. The very way he sat, unbent, feet firmly planted on the floor, ice-cube eyes a cold azure, was a double-dare. He was an enigma that first day, and although he played a major part in our camp life, I never did find out much about him. His name was Erwin Neidhart. Rumors had it that he was a communist union organizer.

Among those I had not seen before was a strikingly handsome man with melancholy eyes and a well-groomed blond moustache above a feminine mouth. His tall figure was wrapped in an ample camel-hair coat, which he held tightly closed as if he felt chilly. He reminded me of the dashing heroes in my short stories.

I was not the only one who found him attractive. When he stood up to smoke a cigarette in the corridor, a plump girl in a peasant blouse joined him. From my seat next to the corridor I could overhear their talk, but was too immersed in my own thoughts to pay much attention. Then I caught a snatch of their conversation that made me listen. It sounded like a dialogue I might use in a story. How does a girl pick up a man? I began scribbling in my notebook as I often did during my stay at Merxplas.

He must have told her about his travels. "I'd like to see the world, too," the girl said eagerly. "I've never been outside Belgium."

He gave a snuffle of amusement. "I wish I could stay here."

She shot an oblique glance at him. Disbelieving. Then: "I was born in Turnhout, the next stop. My father has a farm here. I'll live here the rest of my life. My name is Lucille Clairmont."

"Mine is Koloman Gal."

"Hungarian?"

"I was born in Budapest."

"But your French is perfect."

"I speak several languages. It's part of my job. I'm an artist."

"Painter?"

"Trapeze artist."

Her eyes widened, blue and thrilled. "How interesting! Where do you go now?"

"Merxplas."

"Merxplas? But that's a tiny village."

"I'm not going to the village. Some camp."

"The vagrant camp?"

"Yes. What's it like?"

"Oh, my goodness, I never was there. It's for all sorts of riffraff. Beggars. People who don't want to work. Criminals. I don't know, really. We pay no attention. Will you perform there?"

"No."

"Visit?"

"No."

"Then why do you go to this godforsaken place?"

"I will be interned there."

"You're kidding."

"Joking is the furthest from my mind."

I stole a glance at him. He was older than I first thought. The lines around his mouth had deepened. His hand that held the cigarette trembled.

The wind from the open window tousled the girl's fine blond hair. She smoothed it away from her forehead. "Did you, uh, do anything?"

He shook his head.

"Then why?" the girl insisted. "Why the vagrant camp?"

He raked his hair with hooked fingers, looking away from her at the passing landscape of fields and little houses. "I gave a substantial contribution to my government," he said. Seeing her confused look, he explained: "When the Austrian government faced the Nazi takeover, it proclaimed a plebiscite to decide whether the Austrians wanted to remain independent—the only way to save the country from the Nazis. The Austrian government asked for campaign contributions. The list of the main contributors is in the hands of the Gestapo. They are arresting the people on that list."

"But why are the Belgians arresting you?"

"Why?" He had spoken without bitterness or self-pity. Now his voice overturned in sudden rage. "I can't answer that. Ask Hitler. Ask the Belgian government. Or the countries that closed their borders. Ask psychologists, economists, politicians, churchmen, or doctors in nut houses."

The girl laughed inappropriately. "And these men?" She jerked her head toward us.

"Vagrants, all of them. A new breed of vagrants. A medical doctor. A judge. A factory owner."

"They must have done..." She hesitated.

"Something wrong? Oh yes. They had jobs the Nazis wanted. Apartments. Shops. Factories. Belonged to organizations the Nazis hated. They are socialists, communists, freemasons. Most of them are Jews."

She still sounded doubtful. "But you are traveling freely."

"Yes, no chains. Over there, by the window, the funny guy with the clown's face, is the watchdog from the Refugee Committee. True, we were not forced. We had a free choice: Merxplas or Germany."

The train clattered over bumpy tracks. A cluster of little houses slid into view. A church. "Turnhout," the girl said. "My stop. Yours, too. The train doesn't go to Merxplas." Tentatively, she added, "I suppose you can write from there?"

"I have no idea. Until two days ago I didn't know this place existed."

She fumbled in her handbag, found a pencil and scribbled on a slip of paper. She tossed back her floppy blond hair and, in a gesture of daring, handed him the note. "Write if I can do anything."

His face reddened with pleasure.

"Number four," Pleienberg read from a list. "Gal, Koloman."

"Here," Gal responded and put the girl's address in his pocket.

She forced a smile and waved with her fingertips.

"You know my name," he said. "And also my number."

He rejoined our group and lifted his little suitcase from the overhead shelf.

Little did I know that I had witnessed the beginning of one of the few happy endings life wrote for the inmates of Merxplas.

3.

Reality awaited us at the railroad station of Turnhout in the form of two men who wore the same uniform as the guards in _Prison a Forest_: trim, dark-blue jackets with silver buttons and flat caps. One was a thick-necked man, squat, with bristly fox-red hair; the other a lanky, long-legged youth with alert blue eyes, hardly older-looking than Fred Glogau. The ox-necked's name was René Dierx. He had watched over the vagrants at Merxplas for eight years and was convinced that people were lazy, stupid, wicked, and could be manipulated only by rewards and punishment. He later told me stories about the inmates whom he always referred as numbers. At Merxplas, they worked for low wages and when they had saved 200 francs they were released. It often took two years or more. Some blew the money in a few days and were returned to the camp. His favorite story was about the old-timer who, when released, bought himself a return bus ticket to Merxplas. Dierx had seen Jews once, in Antwerp, black-clad bearded men in long caftans, skull caps, and curls at their temples. He never quite believed we were real Jews.

The younger man's name was Albert Lebret. He was fresh out of school and received his basic training at Merxplas. He believed people were people. I suspect his training was entirely unsuited for his future career although it may have helped him in life.

Pleienberg apologized to Dierx for not having our own transportation. "For the next transport we'll have our own bus," he promised.

When can we expect the next transport?" Dierx asked.

"In a few days. Our people are eager to get to this haven."

"We're not really prepared. The orders came so suddenly. There's lots of work to do."

"Work doesn't scare us," Benedikt said. "We haven't had anything to do for months, Mr. ..."

"The inmates call me *chef*," Dierx said curtly.

"Great," Benedikt said. "We lost our jobs. Now at least we have a *chef*."

Which, I knew from my high school French, didn't mean cook, but boss.

Dierx's expression showed that he found this kind of dialogue completely inappropriate. He herded us into a little bus with barred windows, the kind that delivers suspects to prison. We got to know it well and called it the "Merxplas Dogcatcher."

4.

We crammed onto the two benches running along the sides of the van. The two guards stood between us, each facing one bench. "All they need is fixed bayonets," grumbled a square-faced man sitting next to me. He was Dr. Theodor Berman, who had been the head of Internal Medicine at the General Hospital in Vienna. He spoke in short, definite sentences, as if giving a diagnosis. Across from me sat a clump-footed, gnomish man, slightly hunched as if forever weary. His name was Peter Kraus, up to last week the owner of a tool-and-die factory in Graz. I looked around. Everybody sat hunched, empty, and weary. Even Benedikt, my role model.

The landscape crept by. Woods, thinning out, meadows, and heath, heath, and more heath. Miles of heath. Then buildings of red brick, little boxes, big boxes, all in the same style, sprinkled throughout the land. Even a brick church with a brick steeple. As a child I had a toy set from which you could build structures such as these. The vagrant camp.

The bus stopped in front of one of two giant brick boxes, fortresses with barred windows, scrubbed clean and well kept. Between the two buildings stretched a grassy space. Behind the first building was a soccer field. At the small ends of the two boxes and the soccer field ran a road from the brick church to a long-stretched building. No walls or barbed wire. The camp was part of the landscape. To escape through those miles of open heath was as promising as a flight through the Sahara.

A blue figure appeared on the road, emerging from the long-stretched building. From his high cylindrical hat I knew this was another *monsieur le directeur*. He had four gold stripes around his hat. The director at *Prison a Forest* had only three.

The Merxplas director was even more smoothly polite than his colleague in Brussels — one gold stripe more. He introduced himself as Director Vandenheuvel and shook hands with each one of us. His wrinkled face, his regretful voice, his mourning eyes all expressed sorrow about what he had to do to us. He explained the layout like a guide on a sight-seeing tour. The brick box in front of us was Pavilion A, reserved for us. He made it sound like a hotel reservation. It would hold 160. The building across the grassy patch was Pavilion B, for the next 160. He pointed with a little Belgian flag to the long-stretched building, the camp administration, off limits to us. The area beyond the church was the vagrants' territory. He called them *personnes sans domicile*, the homeless. Although we were part of the *colonie de bienfaisance*, under his jurisdiction, we had nothing to do with the "homeless," we were not to mix with them. While he was talking, a column of dark, decrepit figures shuffled by in the distance, carrying spades and scythes.

"They're less homeless than we," murmured Waniek.

With a winsome gesture host Vandenheuvel invited us into Pavilion A. Each of us carried his suitcase with his earthly riches. I also carried my precious typewriter.

We were led into an enormous hall, taking up the entire width and almost half the length of the building. Cement ceiling, floor, walls. Long benches and tables along the walls. Windows high up, crisscrossed by bars. Two iron stoves stretching up their black flues like imploring arms. In this barren and barred room, director Vandenheuvel changed from host to bureaucrat. His voice echoed in that bleak cavity when he read our names from a list Pleienberg handed him. Each man whose name was called had to line up along a wall.

"Inventory of the rejects," whispered Peter Kraus who knew about the ways of merchandising.

We formed a lonely line in that empty hall. Only two weeks later it would be filled to desperation with 160 shouting, shoving, shuffling specimens of humanity.

5.

The guards led us upstairs. The entire second floor was taken up by four dormitories, forty beds in each. The walls reached up to arches forming connecting openings between the dorms. My childhood toys had such arched pieces, too. In Merxplas, under each arch, an uplifting moral was painted in Flemish. Over my bed it said, "Virtue has its own rewards." Judge Stein placed his suitcase on a cot under the saying, "Do justice, and justice will be done to you." The cots were the same as in *Prison a Forest*. Iron bedsteads, straw mattresses, straw pillows, army blankets folded neatly. Chef Dierx demonstrated how to fold and tuck them in every morning.

The beds lined up along the walls, about four feet apart. There was no other furniture. Dr. Berman surveyed the room as he might have done as chief surgeon in his Vienna hospital. "Enough beds for an epidemic," he announced in his deep, resonant voice. "And a room cold enough to start one." He dropped his suitcase on a cot under the archway that said, "Save today and you will prosper tomorrow." He collapsed on his cot, suddenly dispirited, forearms on knees, hands dangling. "We do have an epidemic—a brown plague." Then, more to himself, he added, "A plague on England!" This startled me and he noticed it. Why would a Hitler refugee curse England? When he saw my surprise, he gave a short laugh, heaved himself to his feet, and changed the subject. "Don't say we have no choices. You can stand your valise next to your bed like a nightstand, or under the bed like a pisspot."

A bell sounded. Lunch time. The meals were cooked by the homeless, Dierx explained. Today the food would be brought to us. Starting tomorrow, we'd have to assign a crew to pick it up from the central camp kitchen.

The guards led us downstairs. In addition to the dayroom where we first assembled, the floor contained a room with school benches and a blackboard, and a dining room with rows of tables and benches. One table was set with plates, forks, spoons, and tin cups. A piece of bread lay on each plate. Next to the table stood two large cauldrons, one filled with black coffee, the other with barley soup. We took turns filling our plates and cups.

"It's a prison," Berman diagnosed, between spoonfuls.

"In the last, godforsaken corner of this phony democracy," Peter Kraus added, his frail body shrinking even lower. "Here we'll go to rot."

"That will depend on us," Benedikt said. "We'll be six hundred. If we pull together they cannot overlook us."

Neidhart, across the table, stared at him in surprise, then looked around and shook his head. "Pie in the sky," he said.

"We can bring it down to earth and divide it," Benedikt said. "Tell me one reason why six hundred people cannot work together."

"Because they are six hundred."

Benedikt leaned forward, intent with his idea. As he talked, his words tumbled from his lips in torrents. As I got to know him better, I loved the youthful enthusiasm that made him speed up his sentences to telegraph style. Often his words could not keep up with his thoughts, and he began to sputter. His eyes widened and his slim fingers gallopped through the air to emphasize a point.

"We'll either rot here or survive," he burbled. "We come from different places — manufacturers, professionals, shopkeepers, clerks. What unites us is that we're in the same boat. We can drift or row. We can do more than feel sorry for ourselves."

"Right," Berman said. "This vegetating as a refugee makes me sick. Might as well do something."

"You can do a lot as a doctor." Benedikt spoke in staccato. "We cannot afford to start our new lives sick. And we'll have to prepare ourselves. Learn languages. New skills. The world doesn't need German-speaking paper shufflers. It needs farmers and carpenters and English-speaking auto mechanics."

Koloman Gal, holding his coffee cup warming both hands around it, volunteered. "I guess my English is good enough to teach until we'll get our English professor."

A quiet, rubber-faced youngster with a turned-up nose cleared his throat and spoke into the momentary silence. "I was a carpenters' apprentice in Wels. Otto Einhorn. If you think…"

"Great." Benedikt tore a page from my notebook and wrote down the name. "Anyone else?"

A boulder of a man said gruffly, "I'm a professional boxer. I suppose that's not a skill you want to learn. But I know something about body work. How about gymnastics in the morning? To keep in shape?"

"Excellent. Name? Max Hutt?" Benedikt added it to his list.

Ludwig Sommer rose ponderously. "I don't want to withhold my special knowledge from you, my comrades in misery," he began what threatened to be a long speech. "You all know that I had the finest salon in Vienna. Of course, it is not possible to teach you this very sophisticated trade in the short time I'll be here, but you can be sure I'll do my best to…"

"Retraining course number two," Benedikt noted down. "Tailoring."

Sommer sat down, pouting. No one else had anything to offer. Teaching short-story writing in German was obviously not what we needed.

"Hey, you," Neidhart called out from across the table. "You have a typewriter. How about putting out a weekly newsletter?"

I was surprised how pleased I was when Benedikt scribbled down the suggestion. I suddenly felt hot and hoped I wasn't blushing. "A little propaganda never hurts," Neidhart added. "I'll give you a hand."

Another moment of silence. Then: "How about a canteen?" Peter Kraus leaned forward, eyes glittering behind heavy glasses. "Cigarettes, chocolates, stamps?"

"Good idea," Benedikt agreed. "A co-op. We pool the money and sell at cost. You want to be in charge?"

Kraus made a thick, strangled sound. "I don't know." He stretched each syllable. "It would leave me no time for retraining. I have to think of my future. And my foot. I have an extra handicap."

"I see." Benedikt tapped his pencil on the table. "Perhaps we can find someone who takes the canteen without making a profit."

"I'll do it." Waniek said it, quietly.

"Don't you want to take retraining?"

"Want to, yes. But it's hopeless. I'm terribly clumsy." He had a frozen smile on his face while he spoke. "I can't hit a nail without banging my fingers. I can think of no trade I could handle. I barely made it to office clerk, with a bit of pull. Selling chocolates and stamps, maybe, in a pinch. Especially if I don't have to figure profits. Playing store would kill time, keep me from thinking."

"You can always change to retraining," Benedikt said. "This is not a job for life."

"Emigration itself is for life," Waniek said, smiling his dreamy, embarrassed smile.

Judge Stein had followed our talk with increasing alertness. He shifted heavily on his seat. He said in his rich, sonorous voice, "What we need are ground rules."

Benedikt looked up. "Laws? A constitution?"

I was not sure if he was facetious. But Stein was serious. He picked up the idea with enthusiasm. "Yes, a constitution. Why not? Hans Kelsen and I often talked about an ideal constitution. He was disappointed with the compromise he had to make."

Kelsen was the jurist who wrote the Austrian Constitution after the First World War. He had been my teacher at the University of Vienna. I found Stein's idea absurd.

"A Constitution of Merxplas," I said aloud.

"Funny," Waniek said gently. "The great democracies go to pot, and here we are talking about establishing one in a vagrant camp."

"What do you propose?" asked Stein.

Waniek wore his smile like a mask. "I can only pick apart. Productive thoughts are not my thing."

6.

In my notebook I find the following comment: "The change is amazing. Like flowers in a meadow, trampled down and rising up again after a shower. Dull faces brighten. A purpose. Hope where there was nothing but despair. I feel it myself. To publish a newsletter for a handful of outcasts—what difference does it make? It makes a difference."

7.

Director Vandenheuvel and Pleienberg entered the dining hall. "Let's go to the library," Pleienberg said. We filed into the room I had considered a classroom. One wall was covered with a shelf of books in French and Flemish. *The Ruler of the Universe* was here, too.

Pleienberg placed himself in front of the blackboard, next to Vandenheuvel who was two heads taller, even without his high hat. We squeezed into the school benches. They were attached to desks with built-in ink pots.

Pleienberg raised himself on tiptoe. Despite his elevator shoes, he didn't gain much on Vandenheuvel. Pleienberg tried in vain to make his squeaky voice sonorous. He started each sentence deep-toned and ended high-pitched. Before each sentence he took a deep breath. He probably took lessons in public speaking.

We were guests of the Belgian government, he said. We ought to show gratitude for that hospitality. We were not part of the reformatory camp but had to follow its general rules, though we were a foreign body in it.

"Even here," Berman murmured. He sat next to me, doodling.

Vandenheuvel recited the rules. It sounded like the list on the walls of my prison cell. He spoke in rapid French, and Pleienberg translated sentence by sentence. Wake, 6 a.m. Make the beds. Walk across to the washrooms in Pavilion B. Breakfast,7:15. Free time between meals. We were to keep floors and tables clean, wash the dishes, heat the stoves. Permission was required to go beyond the designated areas. Lunch at 12, dinner at 6. Bed time 8:30, lights out at 9, after 9:30 absolute silence.

"At all times, follow the chef's orders," Vandenheuvel con-cluded. "That's all, gentlemen." He put on his high hat, nodded pleasantly, and left.

"Here go our plans." Hutt hit the air with an angry uppercut.

I felt like I was hit myself. We all sat in our school benches, two rows of dunces flunked out of life. The hopeful flowers had wilted.

Neidhart grunted his large frame out of the space between school bench and desk. He sat down on top of his desk, legs dangling. "Okay, babes," he grinned through his gold teeth. "You thought you tumbled right into paradise. Well, you got kicked out. There's work to do. The sweat of the brow, and all that."

"Mr. Pleienberg," Benedikt said. "we'd like to talk things over."

Pleienberg looked uncomfortable. "What kinds of things?"

"We have some autonomy within the camp rules. In fact, our separation from the rest of the camp commits us to some form of self-government." Pleienberg's expression of discomfort deepened as he listened to Benedikt's cascade of ideas. "Language courses, retraining—fine." He dragged his word. "But what do you mean by self-government?"

"We'll elect our own representatives. Spokesmen to Vandenheuvel and the Refugee Committee."

Pleienberg shook his head emphatically. "No, no. That won't work. The Committee has an obligation to the government. To coordinate things."

"That might lead to trouble." I admired Benedikt. He was a skillfully advocating our case without antagonizing Pleienberg. "The staff on the Committee are refugees like us. They are free, we are not. Our people here will ask by what right some refugees can tell others what to do." He took a deep breath, looking pensive. "We had a dream. The victims of a dictatorship holding up the banner of democracy."

"The Belgian press will take note of that." Neidhart threw that in, a random remark.

Pleienberg squinted at him. A ponderous furrow appeared on the little man's forehead.

Neidhart pressed his point. "Belgium is a democracy. Your idea will impress them."

Pleienberg looked startled. He took off his glasses and nibbled the end of the stem. Neidhart knew he had scored and unashamedly put it on thickly.

"The press knows you established the Committee. You got the government to offer this camp as a humanitarian solution. Merxplas is a social experiment. Now it's going to be a political experiment as well."

Whatever Neidhart's background was, he knew his politics—and would-be politicians. Pleienberg leaned against the teacher's table, took out his purple handkerchief, and cleaned his glasses for what seemed to be ages. Then he put his glasses back on again and said in his strident voice: "I'll think about it. We do need a spokesman who directly reports to the Committee. One of you, but appointed by the Committee." His glance skimmed our group. It rested briefly on Benedikt, Stein, Berman, even on me. Then, abruptly, "Would Mr. Holländer be acceptable?"

Holländer startled to attention, blushing up to his receding red hair.

"He's the oldest among you," Pleienberg said. "Experienced. Army veteran. He'll work with those you'll elect. Agreed?"

Some of us nodded, emptily. Benedikt was about to speak but kept silent.

"Kissing ass pays off," Waniek mumbled next to me.

"Well, Mr. Holländer," Pleienberg addressed him directly. "Your colleagues have chosen you. Do you accept?"

Holländer stood at attention, then bowed. "It's an honor," he stammered.

"So, that's settled." Pleienberg withdrew behind a posture of military efficiency. "In a few days I'll bring the next transport. You can then report to me what you've worked out." He pulled out a pocket watch and clicked it open. "I'm quite sure you'll get adjusted."

He nodded briskly and left. I felt drained.

Not Benedikt. He stood erect, spine straight, chin lifted, eyes widening in excitement. "Now we'll see what we can do with our Merxplas experiment."

Chef Dierx entered the room. "Men," be bellowed, "There are things to do. Fetch water, wash the dishes, start the ovens. Dinner bell is at six. At 5:30 two of you go to the camp kitchen and get the food. I'll show them where. The guards' room is right next to the dining hall."

Neidhart slapped Holländer's back. "Mr. President," he roared. "What do you want us to do first? Write the Constitution or wash the dishes?"

Holländer looked scared. Benedikt assigned the jobs. I split wood and started a fire in the potbellied stove. Then I got my typewriter from under my cot and went to the empty schoolroom. I typed out a story about an aging president of a small country. One afternoon the police arrested a dozen vagrants who paraded in front of the president's villa, shouting "Remember November second!" which was only a week away. The riffraff also carried signs with the same message. When police tried to disperse them, saying that political demonstrations were not permitted, they insisted they did not know what it was all about, they were hired by friends of the president. It turned out that the president was married to a young wife but often got so absorbed in the affairs of state that he forgot their wedding anniversary—November second.

III. The First Revolt

1.

Now a word about myself.

I was born Josef Epstein. My father had been director of the municipal warehouses of Vienna, forced into early retirement after the government takeover by Dollfus and his Austro-fascists in 1934 when most Jews were removed from responsible government positions. After his retirement my father helped me type the stories I wrote with my friend Max, under the common pen name Peter Fabrizius. I shortened the name to the more pronounceable Fabry when I arrived in the United States. My mother was a full-time mother and wife, and the unassuming centerpiece of a family of about 25, all living within easy commuting by streetcar.

I am an irremediable optimist. I didn't know it then, in Merx-plas, at age 29, because the Ruler of the Universe had been very kind to me, and you don't know you're an optimist until you get clobbered. Since Hitler had become the protector of the Aryan race in Austria earlier that year, I had been the recipient of clobberings which continued for quite a few more years. During that time, many realists warningly pointed out my penchant for optimism. I now admit I am one. My optimism has tripped me up many times, but it also saved me from anxiety and despair, perhaps saved my sanity, possibly my life.

Anyway, there is not much I can do about it. I believe we are born either optimists or pessimists. I also believe in another distinction over which we *do* have some control: we are either futurists, here-and-nowers, or crabs. I am an optimistic futurist. Jakob Benedikt belonged to that clan, too. Optimistic futurists get clobbered like anyone else, but they go to great lengths scratching the dirt to find some little treasure they can use in the future.

Judge Stein was an optimistic here-and-nower. He believed in truth and justice, and remained their interpreter under all circumstances, even in an age of lies and injustice. He kept working on a constitution for an ideal republic in a camp for vagrants.

Herbert Waniek was a pessimistic here-and-nower. He was convinced that everything would come out badly in the end and we had to keep busy to prevent ourselves from thinking about it. Running the canteen gave him the opportunity to observe his fellow earthlings with gentle sarcasm.

Most of the others were crabs. They kept looking back onto a past when they had families, careers, property, ambitions. They were either optimistic crabs who gained strength from past achievements, or pessimistic crabs who used the past to find excuses for present and future failures.

2.

As an optimistic futurist, I was additionally blessed with an active imagination. I imagined future catastrophes, not to scare myself but to work out scenarios of how to deal with them. Many of my humorous short stories developed from such imaginary ramblings about mishaps. Much of what is seen as humorous begins with a slip on a banana peel or a pie in the face. As to my own life, I can see now that many of my imagined catastrophes never happened, and when they occurred, were not as bad as I visualized, and if they were bad, I had imagined ways to deal with them.

Also, I have this curious capacity of splitting my experiences. I am doing something odd, or uncomfortable, or scary, and also see myself from the outside, as an audience sees an actor on the stage. For instance, there I am in Merxplas at six o'clock in the morning, assigned to start a fire in the two iron stoves in the dayroom so the herd of human buffalos would find a half-heated place when they come storming in after breakfast, all 160 of them. The wood is chopped and piled next to the stove, but I need paper to start the fire. I ransack every corner but finally have to go to the last resort: the Flemish books in the library. I know the collection had been depleted by previous frustrated fire builders, and I grab one of the remaining volumes. My assigned partner this morning is Josef Klingenberg, recently professor of philosophy at the University of Freiburg. He is lumpish, with a waddling gait and waggling jowls, wattles, and cheeks, given to stalking about, hands clasped in the back, head bowed in thought. He is unhappy about my choice of Aristotle's *Ethics* as kindling and begs me to spare the book. I argue that no one in the camp will ever read Aristotle in Flemish, and that a warm dayroom under the circumstances is the good and the beautiful in the best Aristotelian sense. And no, using the book for starting the fire is *not* comparable to Nazi book burning. At the same time I see this scene as part of a cabaret skit, or the seed of a short story, or simply as an amusing anecdote to be told later in a cricle of friends. I let Klingenberg keep Aristotle, and we tear up *The Churches of Ghent.*

3.

Pavilion A filled up quickly. The second transport brought 54 men, the third 48. They filled almost three of the four dorms of the building. The Committee had rented a van, the Merxplas Dogcatcher Number Two.

The newcomers found the big brick box no longer a cold, echoing cavity full of confused hopelessness. Judge Stein had drafted emergency ordinances, Benedikt negotiated with Van-denheuvel about granting us some self-government, and I had produced our first newsletter. Actually, I had done little more than type on my portable what Neidhart dictated. We had two copies. One was pinned on a bulletin board in the dayroom, the other in the library. There was always a jumble of men clustered in front of them. Neidhart knew his stuff. The sheet was a morale booster. We were the pioneers of a great experiment, it said. On our success depended the future of hundreds of refugees stranded in Belgium. Merxplas provided a shelter until overseas visas could be secured. I felt the propaganda working on me. I had a mission. Typing that news sheet seemed the most im-portant writing I'd ever done.

The bulletin board also displayed handwritten announcements. "Morning gymnastics, daily 7 a.m. on the soccer field. Trainer: M. Hutt." "English for Beginners, 4 p.m. in the Library, Koloman Gal." "Want to retrain for carpentry? Speak to Einhorn."

The requisition of the bulletin board was my triumph. I had spoken to Albert Lebret, the young guard, and he had allowed me to go to the garbage dump behind the Administration Building where I found a large empty cardboard box. We used two sides of it for the two bulletin boards. Holländer asked me for a piece of the third side, on which he printed the block letters SECRETARIAT. He proudly hung the sign on the door of a cubby hole that had been so designated by Vandenheuvel. Even skeptical Herbert Waniek was caught by the flutter of excitement when he was allowed to convert a broom closet into a canteen. He enlisted Otto Einhorn to construct a sales counter from some loose boards. Now Waniek sat behind the counter in the empty closet, scribbling down orders for merchandise Pleienberg would eventually bring. Many projects were no more than hopes by optimistic futurists. Most ambitious was Dr. Berman's request for a doctor's office, with space for a few beds.

The new arrivals were checked off a list by Vandenheuvel and catalogued by Bernhard Klein, whose painstaking handwriting would have done honor to a medieval monk. Klein was a quiet, thin man with a mighty forehead and a scraggly crown of graying hair around a bald plate. He had been a dealer in antiques in Vienna. When a horde of Nazi vandals stormed his shop and smashed everything in sight, the Nazi commissar called Klein to account because the store contained shambles instead of precious vases and rare books. The commissar had intended to appropriate the store for himself and filed a criminal suit against Klein, so Klein had to flee to escape punishment for a crime committed against him.

Klein, in his fine bookkeeper's penmanship, entered the name of each new arrival on a list, gave him a number, and noted skills of potential teachers. The two new transports brought teachers in watch repairing, auto mechanics, electrical work, sausage making, barbering, and brick laying. We also found a man who could teach Spanish and a replacement for Gal to teach English. Vandenheuvel set aside land for farming where we could grow our own vegetables. As a teenager, Gal had helped his uncle on the Hungarian puszta raise hogs. He and a dozen others wanted to learn about agriculture, useful overseas. Rumor had it that British Guiana was admitting immigrants to clean its swamps. Bolivia was said to be looking for people to turn jungle into farmland.

Each new arrival was handed a "Merxplas uniform" worn by the vagrants: a dark blue sack-cloth jacket, a pair of jeans, and a beret. Most of us had only one, at most two, suits. The camp clothes were welcome because they saved our wardrobe for our start in life somewhere overseas. It was Waniek's first job to hand out these clothes to the new arrivals as they passed his still-empty canteen.

Among the newcomers I recognized Siegfried Neumann, a comedian from one of the little cabarets for which I had written an occasional skit. He was a tall, gawky man, his wrists and ankles protruding from the sleeves and pants of the largest Merxplas uniform Waniek could find. There was a saying in Vienna that a comic, to be successful, must be tall and thin, short and fat, or have talent. Neumann was tall and thin.

When he spotted me, his face lit up, and he immediately suggested we start a cabaret. "Listen," he bubbled, "I know dozens of the funniest skits by Farkas and Grünbaum, and you can write new ones about this hellhole." Farkas and Grünbaum were two well-known Jewish comics who wrote their own material for Vienna's best-known cabaret, the Simpl. Neuman jerked a quick thumb toward the dayroom. "These men need some cheering up. They look like the bottom of the human garbage pail. Maybe they are. But they don't need wallow in self-pity. I've seen cheerier faces at funerals. Let's see if we can find some talents among these beagle heads."

The idea appealed to me but I had doubts if the bottom of a human garbage pail was a suitable place for a cabaret.

I was wrong.

4.

The second and third transports had arrived already on the Committee's own Merxplas Dogcatcher Number Two. Pleienberg, too, had been on board. With the fourth transport, he drove his own car and brought his wife. I saw her from the distance as I talked cabaret fantasies with Siegfried Neumann. She was shiveringly wrapped in a fur coat, and attached to her hat was a veil that covered her face down to the tip of her nose.

The dayroom was a preview of things to come, bubbling with edgy, irritable, and frustrated human beings. They felt discarded and filled their emptiness with cacophonous chatter. We were now more than a hundred and had to outshout each other. A few here-and-nowers were playing cards. The pessimistic crabs, the vast majority, talked about what they had lost and about their futureless future. They were worried about those they had left behind and fearful of what lay ahead. This was the constituency of our hatching republic. They didn't care about constitutions, and retraining for tailors or barbers was as far from their minds as the moon. Or so I thought.

I was wrong again.

5.

But first it got worse.

At the noon bell, we crammed into the dining hall and perched on the narrow benches along the tables, six men per bench. Our kitchen crew wheeled in the soup tank and Albert Lebret, in his Flemish-tinted German, choreographed the flow of the hungry between tables and soup tank. The prominent presence of two uniformed guards visibly depressed the newcomers. The buzz in the room sparked with irritation.

I sat with my friends from the pioneer transport. Pleienberg and his wife joined us. She was beautiful, cool, and regal like a painting by Gustav Klimt, with the classical profile of Nofretete. "President" Holländer assiduously brought them their plates of soup. He truly was a president in quotes. Decisions were made by Vandenheuvel and Pleienberg.

The soup was barley broth with floating pieces of potatoes, carrots, and threadlets of meat.

"Delicious," Pleienberg said after the first spoonful. "Isn't it, Helen?"

She nodded while she went through the pretense of dipping her spoon into the liquid in front of her and wrapping her pretty lips around it.

"The soup isn't bad," Benedikt said. "But the same, day after day. And potatoes at night. What do you think, Berman?"

"In the long run insufficient," Berman diagnosed. "We need supplements."

"I don't know how we can do it," Pleienberg said with a touch of impatience. "Dozens of refugees come across the border every day. Our resources are strained to the limit."

"We are preparing ourselves for a new life overseas," Judge Stein interjected. "We have to be in good health."

I became aware that it had become quiet in the hall. Those at the other tables were trying to listen in. Pleienberg, too, knew he had an audience.

"I've discussed the diet with Dr. Jan Bruining, the camp physician," he declared with conspicuous kindness. "He assured me the food contained everything the body requires. After all, the homeless have lived on it for years."

"Look at them," Berman growled. "Pale, gaunt figures; dead eyes. One can live for years with stomach ulcers. When you drive back, look to the left behind the church. The camp cemetery. A sea of crosses."

Pleienberg puffed through his nostrils. His mustache bristled. "You didn't expect this to be a sanatorium? It's a place to protect you from being shipped back to Germany. It's certainly better than a concentration camp."

At the mention of this word a rumbling rolled through the dining hall.

Benedikt's eyes widened in resentment. Sitting next to him I saw his jaw muscles work in restraint. "No, we don't expect a sanatorium. All we ask for are small supplements. Sugar for the coffee. A sausage. A herring."

Some of the men clapped. Pleienberg's baby face became apoplectic. "That's what I get for granting you self-determination. I knew it. Offer a little finger and you want the whole hand. A little understanding, please!"

"That's what we ask from you." Benedikt struggled mightily to sound calm. "We've mentioned only the most urgent needs."

"Oh, there is more?"

"I don't know how we can have retraining without tools, language courses without books, a canteen without supplies. You have established this camp..."

"I wish I hadn't." Pleienberg murmured these words as if to himself but they reverberated throughout the room. He reacted to the rumble of resentment with a gesture of annoyance. "Those who were shipped back know."

Neidhart, at the next table, jerked to his feet. He pointd a forefinger at Pleienberg like a sword. "You've got no right to threaten us with Germany," he shouted. "Not you, a refugee yourself!"

I sat only five feet away from Pleienberg but even I could not hear his reply in the sudden uproar. A match had been dropped into a cinderbox of emotions. Mild-mannered shopkeepers, clerks, and businessmen leaped to their feet and shook their fists. Benedikt climbed on the table and waved his arms in a vein attempt to calm them down. The two guards bravely waded into the swirl. Their presence only seemed to feed the fury. I remember my anguished thought: Now all is lost.

At that moment Helen Pleienberg stood up. Slowly she rose, slim, blond, well-groomed in her slithery silken dress that matched her turquoise eyes. Wide-looped earrings, a torrent of necklaces . She stood silent, neither angry nor conciliatory, simply waiting. The shouting quieted down.

"I'll establish a women's auxiliary," she announced in the sudden hush. "We'll raise money to get what you need."

Cheers flared as spontaneously as the boos before. The men at the far end of the hall climbed on the tables to see the woman. But she had sat down again, took out a mirror and carefully painted her lips on the ivory mask of her face.

She put away her mirror and snapped shut her handbag. She turned to Benedikt and said in her light, lilting voice: "Make a list of what you need."

The bell ended the lunch hour. The guards, obviously relieved, motioned the crowd out the doors. Pleienberg, with teacher's pet Holländer in his rear, left. Helen remained seated for her private conversation with Benedikt. He flicked a glance at me, signaling me to stay and take notes. The woman completely ignored me. Once she looked in my direction, right through me as if I were air. Benedikt listed our needs. Extra food, coal, textbooks, office supplies, material for our courses. Nails, hammers, needles and thread, electrical wiring, scissors, razors. "I'll ask the teachers of the courses what they need. You think you might get us an old car for our class in auto mechanics?"

She didn't answer directly. "My husband brought a few things," she said. "Cigarettes, writing paper, chocolate bars, a soccer ball."

Benedikt's eyes widened again. This time in surprise. "Why didn't he say so? Why all this wrangling?"

The woman laughed. It wasn't a mirthful laugh. "His way of doing things. You'll get used to it. I also brought something. Vases."

"Vases?"

"It's nice to have flowers on the tables."

Benedikt fumbled for words. She added: "It will improve the atmosphere."

"I'm not sure. Vases on tables where there is no sugar for coffee? It would be resented."

"I think flowers are important."

"Only for people with full bellies."

She gave no indication that she had heard. She got up and lowered the veil from the rim of her hat. She looked at Benedikt through its mesh as through a lorgnon. We others did not exist. I smelled trouble.

This time I was right.

6.

The pessimists predicted Helen Pleienberg would have forgotten about us as soon as she got into her car. The optimists were cautiously hopeful.

This time the optimists won. A few days later, Merxplas dogcatcher number two brought a whole flea market of used tools, laxatives, bandages, razor blades, cigarettes, writing paper, stamps, and cough drops. An old car for the would-be auto mechanics was on the way, we were told, but had broken down thirty kilometers from Brussels.

Waniek fretfully watched as the shelves of his cubbyhole were being thinly stocked. "What do I do now?" he groaned in mock disappointment. "Now I have no more excuse not to sell anything."

Dr. Berman took inventory of the medical supplies. "Now I can cure anything," he announced, "that can be fixed with aspirin and a band aid. For Merxplas, this is a medical advance on the level of the discovery of X-rays. Up to now, all I could tell my patients was to wash their hands and stop smoking. They didn't have any cigarettes anyway."

The most popular item of the shipment was a barrel of dried herrings, a welcome supplement of the daily bread-soup-coffee menu. The strangest item was an accordion. Siegfried Neumann pounced at it as soon as it was lifted from the van. "Anyone know how to play this thing?"

A lanky, downy-cheeked youngster from the newest trans-port grabbed the accordion and played the Blue Danube waltz. I was embarrassed to feel a lump in my throat. I looked around. A lot of clapping, cheering, and singing. In Vienna, we were spat upon, beaten, kicked out, and here we reacted with nostalgia to that unofficial Viennese anthem. The music of childhood!

After the clapping died down, a squeaky voice brayed:

"Hitler and Goering
don't eat dry herring."
We looked around. "Who was that?" asked Neumann.
No answer. The youngster put his accordion down, took out a handkerchief, knotted it, and draped it over his forefinger.
"I'm Hanky-Panky," the squeaky voice said while the handkerchief puppet waggled its knotted head.
"Are you a ventriloquist, too?" Siegfried Neumann peered nearsightedly at the handkerchief.
Hanky-Panky jerked its head toward the youngster. "Not I," he screeched. "*He* is."
Neumann who had scouted each incoming transport for talent, so far with little success, beamed. "Can you accompany me to 'Let Me Kiss Your Hand, Madame'?
The youngster went through a pantomime of resignation and picked up the accordion. "I'd rather kiss your ass," he groaned.
The quicksilvery boy with the impudent smile turned out to be a great find. His name was Franz Jäger, 23. He rattled off a string of jobs he had held: stable boy, milkman, bar pianist, street musician, longshoreman's aid, extra. "I even helped pull the swan in Lohengrin."
Jäger radiated noisily extrovert optimism. He turned to Neumann. "Come on, lets give these basset heads some more Schmaltz."
They sang a few popular hits to a gratefully responsive audience. Neumann, pleased with himself, took repeated bows, going through the routine of crediting his accompanist, blowing kisses, pantomiming exhaustion before agreeing to an encore. Then pudgy Otto Einhorn did some rubber-limbed tap dancing, and the irrepressible Jäger played a medley of folksongs, and we all sang along, discarded people singing the tunes of their evictors. Finally a pale and puckered Peter Kraus stepped for-ward and announced: "I will now sing a serious song."
Without accompaniment he sang the ballad of a mother whose child had been taken from her. The song ended on a high, mellow note. The solemn silence that followed was torn by a muffled moan that seemed to be making its painful way from a shattered heart. Bernhard Klein, his thin body folded like a melted candle, his head collapsed on his limp forearms on the table, sobbed savagely.
His story was passed on in a whisper. His mother, old and paralyzed, knew that her son stayed in Vienna because of her. She managed to drag her body to the window and let herself drop down. In a farewell note she implored him to flee. Klein followed that last motherly advice. One day later the SS came to arrest him for "willful destruction of (his own) property." His mother had given him his life for the second time.
I thought of my own mother, marked with the yellow star of David, a prey of pitiless hunters. Most of the others sat hunched, defeated, staring blindly at images only they could see. Mothers in attics, deprived of their families. In England, on servants' visas, the only kind granted, hoping to secure visas for their husbands in concentration camps. These were the "lucky" ones. Most mothers still were home which had become a death trap.
A sonorous voice floated into the stillness, vibrant with emotion. Professor Klingenberg stood erect, in his ill-fitting Merxplas blues, his deep-set eyes above his paunchy cheeks burning with manic energy. He had let his beard grow and shifted his vagabond beret back from his forehead to the top of his egghead, to serve as a yarmulka.
"Baruch atoh adonai melech ho-oulum she outsi-onu mei atos lechelus go-el Israel."

The deep, throaty voice filled every corner of the silence. The sobbing faded. I myself felt strangely comforted by this blessing which I understood only in part. I had gone to the synagogue on Jewish high holidays and knew that the words "baruch atoh adonai" preceded every prayer, from blessings of the wine to benedictions over a new-born child. I asked Berman who sat next to me on the bench along the wall if he knew what the entire phrase meant. He translated with bitter explicitness:

"Blessed be the Lord, our God, King of the Universe, who led us from slavery to freedom, redeemer of Israel."

Berman kept his head high in rebellious defiance. Most of the men sat in prayerful surrender. I felt the puzzling split in myself: the irony of praising the Ruler of the Universe for his guidance to freedom, and the inexplicable comfort I received from these inappropriate words.

Klingenberg still stood, lips slightly moving. Berman took out his pocket watch and demonstratively snapped it open. He tapped it as he might have tapped the back of a patient. Only later I learned that the same events that had made Klingenberg religious turned Berman into a proud agnostic.

The shrill bell called us to kitchen service.

7.

After dinner I sneaked into the cranny behind our own newly established makeshift kitchen where four huge garbage cans awaited the daily pickup. I always kept my eyes open for relatively quiet places, and the garbage nook qualified as soon as the cans were filled after meals.

I placed my portable typewriter on one of the lids and, standing up, typed a short story about a holdup man who threatened his victim in an empty alley when a voice in no uncertain terms ordered him to drop his gun. His victim's screams attracted a policeman who handcuffed the robber and took out his report book. The robber was puzzled because he could not see anyone who could have scared him enough to drop his gun. He heard the policeman ask his victim for the data.

"Name?"

"George Simper."

"Profession?"

"Ventriloquist."

IV. A Community of Rejects

1.

My own position in the camp perplexed me. Strangers sought me out and told me their life stories, often in embarrassing detail —about a child who died, a friend who had betrayed them, a parent they had left behind. They told me about possessions that were taken from them—a villa, a business, collections, heirlooms. They told me about fortunes they had hid "until all this is over," tricks of survival, cliffhanger escapes, and miraculous rescues.

I listened to their laments, memories, boasts. True, I encour-aged them. All they needed for encouragement was for me to listen. My snoopery was based on the hope of finding ideas for short stories. Perhaps my typewriter attracted them. They threw stories at me as people throw coins into a wishing well. Overnight they had become nobodies. They wanted to be some-body again, even if only through their misadventures. Some even said so. "Listen, you won't believe what I went through. You can write a book about it."

I could have, indeed. A decameron of Western civilization anno 1938. But there was no market for it. Our English readers wanted stories of love and outwitted tricksters, with snappy dialogues and happy endings. The stories I heard had no happy endings, unless you call finding shelter in a camp for vagrants a happy ending. And yet, it was happy compared to those who didn't make it.

Take the story of Heinrich Lobositz, a prickly hedgehog of a man who spoke with bitter vehemence about how he lost his restaurant in Vienna. One of his regular customers had brought a friend from Tyrol. The visitor had a little suitcase but no money, and Lobositz let him stay a few days in a backroom. He showed up again after the Nazi takeover, decked out like a vaudeville general. He had been chief of an illegal bombing squad and his suitcase had contained fourteen kilos of ecrasit. He "aryanized" the restaurant by taking it over, including cash, bank accounts, and valuables. But he was a "good" Nazi. He helped Lobositz cross the border to Mussolini's Italy. This certainly would have been a "good deed" for most other refugees because, at that time, Italy did not yet round up Jews and ship them to death camps. But Lobositz had a paralyzed daughter in Vienna and decided to go back to help her. So he crossed back illegally while others crossed just as illegally in the opposite direction. Lobositz knew he took a great risk when he appealed to the vaudeville general for help. There was no chance of moving his daughter. Lobositz revealed the existence of a hidden vault with valuables, and the Nazi bombing expert entered into a magnanimous agreement: he would let the daughter stay in the little back room, on condition that Lobositz immediately leave Austria. Lobositz crossed Lake Constance in a row boat but was returned to Austria by Swiss guards. He tried Luxembourg and France in vain and finally succeeded in Belgium—until the police arrested him and took him to Merxplas.

Then there was the tale of Georg Kellner, vice-president of the Rothschild Bank in Frankfurt. He was taken to the Dachau concentration camp and released against his promise to turn over his possessions and leave the country within a week. He was a skinny, lost little man who told me how lucky he was to hear of a scheme that worked for a while. At Nassweiler on the French-German border was a Jewish cemetery. The border line ran right through the middle of the cemetery. You climbed over the wall in Germany and climbed over another wall in France. This escape was possible for a short time until this macabre mousehole was plugged. Kellner succeeded while the flight was still possible. "Strange," he said with a rueful smile, "the dead are honored or cursed, depending on which side of the cemetery they are buried."

Escape tricks were discovered, passed on, sold, and foiled. The drain pipe at Lustenau worked for a while. Max Hutt, our fitness trainer, told me about it. At Lustenau the Rhine River separates Austria from Switzerland. Of course, all bridges were guarded but a weak point was discovered. On the stretch where the Rhine used to curve toward Austria a canal was cut to have the river flow in a straight line while the border ran along the old river bed. Thus the area between the canal and the old river bed was Swiss territory. A bridge across the Rhine was unguarded at that point because both ends lay in Switzerland. A person who crossed the old river bed could simply walk across the bridge. But crossing the old bed was impossible because it was a deep swamp. A cement pipe drained some of the water from the swamp. Rumors had it that the pipe was wide enough for a person to crawl through. It was not entirely filled with water. In the middle of the pipe, halfway across, a metal grid blocked the way but early discoverers of that escape route had cut a hole in it. When Hutt reached the grid he found that the hole was too tight for his squat torso to squeeze through but, as he proudly told me, he was strong enough to bend the iron bars. He arrived in Switzerland drenched, muddy, but a free man. Not for long. A friend in Rorschach gave him dry clothes but he was arrested by the Swiss police. Once more he escaped and made his way through France to Belgium.

The pilgrimage escape was told to me by Dr. Willy Kruger, a fragile youngster with fluttering gestures, a quick tremulous smile, and a voice that was fresh and young. In the camp he became Dr. Berman's assistant and friend. Kruger had just finished medical school and married his high school sweetheart Susi, the reason for his hasty flight. According to the Nazi Nuremberg laws, his marriage made him a racial rapist because his wife was Catholic. But her religion, which marked both as criminals, also saved their lives. This is the story he told me:

Susi's aunt was a sister in the Salesian order. She knew of a statue of Mary said to have healing powers enshrined near Walheim in Germany. The shrine was so close to the Belgian border that worshippers regularly went on a pilgrimage from near–by Belgian villages to pray there. The border region was now swarming with fugitives and the priest at Walheim had devised a holy escape route. Whenever a group of Belgian pilgrims came to his little church, he persuaded a few to stay in Walheim and replaced them on the way back with the same number of Jews. Since pilgrimages had been going on for years, the border officials simply waved through the participants, only counting their numbers. And so, Kruger and his wife found themselves one October evening walking slowly, on crutches and wrapped in black hooded cloaks, like the other returning wor-shippers crossing the border—the slowest escape in my notes. The ruse was discovered soon after and the priest taken to a concentration camp.

"Justice prevailed," Berman snorted. "According to the Nuremberg laws."

2.

Judge Stein worked on his Constitution. He sat at a table in the dayroom, oblivious of the maelstrom of shouting, bubbling, blatant men swirling around him. His massive shoulders were hunched over books he had been able to get through Pleienberg. His blunt fingers kept writing, crossing out, annotating, his nutcracker jaw set in determination. The Merxplas Constitution took his mind off his worry about his son who was half Jewish staying with his "Aryan" mother. Stein hoped the boy was safe but had no direct news from him. Stein's wife had stopped even the cryptic messages she had sent before. The only news he received were puzzling and contradictory messages from former neighbors.

My own part in drafting the Merxplas Constitution was undeservedly prominent. Thanks to my typewriter I was to "promulgate" the new law. But there was more to my pro-mine-nce. The first transport to the camp had included three Doctors of Law: Stein, Benedikt, and me. I didn't know much at that time about the framers of the American Constitution, but now I suspect that in Stein's mind we played parts akin to Madison, Franklin, and Hamilton. Stein was obsessed with establishing a perfect union in this camp of have-beens. Benedikt showed interest, but more in the human than the legal aspects. And I? For me, the drafting of the Merxplas Constitution was, at best, an idea for a cabaret sketch.

Stein insisted we hold regular meetings to discuss the legal points he had worked out. Benedikt listened to his studious arguments with absent-minded cordiality.

"Listen," he told me after one of those sessions. "You must help me."

"How?"

"We are not in ancient Athens. We are not the thirteen colonies. Not even a moribund republic like Austria. We are in a prison. Everything we do has to be approved by Vandenheuvel. We are stuck with a nonremovable president with the spine of a jellyfish, and at the mercy of a power-hungry pipsqueak and his snobbish wife. The Merxplas experiment is bound to fail."

I had no answer. It was a Greek tragedy rather than a cabaret sketch.

But Benedikt's here-and-now optimism won out. "What we need," he blurted, eyes flashing, "is not a convention but a community."

I didn' t understand.

"In Frankfurt I worked with refugees from the Russian revolution. That's how I met Natascha. These people didn't need my legal advice. They needed someone to talk to. Emigration is a series of deaths. Of one's country. One's family. Friends. Career. Language. One's usefulness. Natascha and the others were alone, torn from their context. The people here at Merxplas have lost their connectedness. What they need is to feel part of something."

"Part of a prison?"

He leaned back and clasped his hands behind his head. "Even that," he said, remembering. "I've seen parolees hankering for their cellmates. Loneliness is worse than the company of jailbirds. Being useless is worse than making brooms at prison wages. Laws can separate. They can also unite. You must help me get Stein make laws that unite."

"How can we do that?" I asked, almost in desperation because I knew he was right. I myself was tortured by the pain of separation.

"I don't know," he sighed tiredly. "Somehow we must make Merxplas, with all its continuous turmoil, a community." His glowing eyes became dreamy as he stared, without seeing, at the soccer field where a game was in progress. "These are people with memories and hopes. They know what it feels like to belong. Now they are rejects. We have to make them feel that they are not cut off. I'll never forget a summer in the Black Forest. I was lying in a meadow, in a community of flowers, insects, birds.

The sky, clouds." He returned to the here-and-now. "You must think of something. You are the one with imagination."

I tried. I really did. But nothing would come. My imagination ran toward the impractical, fictional, with snappers at the ending that made everything come out well. A Snow–White world. When I saw Judge Stein, reading his drafts to us, his hands fumbling for truth and justice, I felt sorry and helpless. I knew he suffered from his powerlessness to help his son. He had known power. He had sent people to prison, set them free, punished and helped; he was a believer in law and order in a world that was increasingly lawless and disorderly. Writing the Constitution of Merxplas gave him a purpose in a world that had lost all purpose. His friendship with Fred Glogau made him feel needed as his son had needed him. This portly man, with his rumpled hair, and the youngster with the cherub face spent much time together, a two–man community of father–son surrogates.

3.

Perhaps this was the solution: to build the Merxplas community out of small personal relationships. Small knots of communality evolved from the tasks to be performed: the men who started up the oven before daybreak; the team carrying the soup cauldron from the camp kitchen to the dining hall; the clean–up crews.

Two dorms were now filled, and there was camaradery among the forty men in each, especially during the half hour between light–out and the guards' orders of night silence. I find the following entry in my notes and I record it here as a sample of the verbal horseplay that went on before sleeping time.

"Silence, please! Silence!" A self–important voice, unmistakably Sommer's: "I have an important piece of information. Our soup, as in all prisons, contains bromides. This has dangerous side effects. It affects the brain."

Unidentified voice: "It worked fast on you, Sommer!"

Sommer: "This is no joking matter!"

Berman: "It does reduce the sex drive."

Neidhart: "Then I'll go on hunger strike!"

Voice, probably Jäger: "I propose we award our comrade from Berlin the title 'morning hour'."

Several: "Why?"

Jäger: "Because he has gold in his mouth." (Refers to the German proverb, "*Morgenstund hat Gold im Mund*" —Morning hours have gold in their mouths.)

Chorus of good–natured boos. Then a voice: "Time for the bromide to take effect. Let's sleep."

Protests, interrupted by a shrill cockadoodledoo, followed by dog barking.

"Now who is this?"

"Siegfried Neumann, of course. What animal would you like to hear now?"

"A canned sardine."

The guard's voice: "Men, it's nine–thirty. No more talk."

4.

But complete night silence was not always enforceable. Insomnia was one problem, nightmares another. We had plenty of reasons to keep awake and many causes for bad dreams. There was hardly a night when someone didn't wake up, screaming;

hardly a day when someone didn't tell me a story fit for a night–mare. During the night they relived the realities of recent days: wading through a river, mother on back; running through the woods, being shot at; watching parents being beaten. Otto Einhorn, the paunchy carpenter, told me how a group of former schoolmates frightened him out of Austria. They marched to his shop, black–booted and swastika-banded, with an ashenfaced neighbor girl in tow. They accused him of racial rape, formed a kangaroo court, and sentenced him to death. He was forced to eat a "last meal" of cabbage and ashes, was blindfolded, stood against a wall, waiting for the charge. The commando was given, he heard the shots, and fainted. When he came to, they were in stitches. It had been a "joke."

Einhorn had become a bedwetter, an unsolvable problem in the camp. Berman was helpless, as in many of the other cases of panic and phobias.

"I can't believe it," Benedikt said. "All you Viennese here and not one psychiatrist. Where is Freud when we need him?"

"Just as well," Berman grumbled. "They would blame our Jewish grandmothers and write scholarly papers about the Red-Ridinghood complex. Give me sleeping pills any time."

5.

Three weeks after our first transport had arrived the Con–stitution was drafted. It had a preamble and sixteen articles. The preamble was written by Benedikt, the articles—with cautious suggestions from Benedikt—by Stein. My part was mostly that of a court clerk. I took everything down in shorthand and typed it up with three copies, one for each of us to study, add, and refine. Carbon papers, by a stroke of luck, had been part of the second shipment of supplies from the women's auxiliary, together with electric wire, nails, shaving cream, pencils, dried peas, and lentils. The automobile was on its way but had broken down again twenty kilometers from Merxplas.

The preamble read:

"We, fugitives from Hitler's savagery, having temporarily lost control over our destiny, establish this community of Merxplas to regain mastery, replace chaos with laws, and assume respon–sibility for our lives. To this end we ordain the following Constitution."

The Constitution placed the weight of governing on elected trustees. The function of the president (Ernst Holländer) was reduced to ceremonials. Each dormitory of forty was to elect two trustees who would become part of a decision–making council. Since 15 dorms were planned, the 30 trustees would elect from their midst an Executive Council of five. In addition, there would be two functional groups: the appointed foremen of service crews, such as cleaning, heating, storage, and policing; and the teachers of retraining courses such as carpenters, cobblers, tailors, electricians, farmers, and of the language classes.

Stein was resistant to giving any governmental say to these merely utilitarian functionaries, but Benedikt slyly convinced him by pointing to such precedent–setting institutions as the medieval guilds. With contagious fervor and conspiratorial twinkle he spoke to me, between sessions with the Judge, about the many puddles of community that would be formed, among foremen and teachers, and also within each group.

"There will be a little brotherhood of farmers," he enthused. "A team of carpenters. A gang of floor sweepers. A class of Spanish students. It won't be family but they will BELONG." He spoke the word in caps.

Benedikt also asked my support for a Camp Council of all elected and appointed officials, and of a semi–annual General Assembly of all inmates.

"Too much chumminess," Stein grumbled but, since I sided with Benedikt, he conceded the democratic principle of being outvoted two to one.

6.

The draft had to be submitted for approval to Vandenheuvel and to the Committee in Brussels. Holländer peered at the pages I had typed, holding them close to his nose, and studied them as if they were a tax return. He wobbled his head in doubt, clacked his tongue in disapproval, and went through a pantomime of heavy thinking.

"The trustees have too much power," he decided eventually. "Director Vandenheuvel will never approve this."

"That's up to him to decide," Benedikt snapped, and Holländer immediately retreated to his apologetic crouch. "You just take it to him."

Holländer was the contact man to Vandenheuvel as well as to Pleienberg. His contact with Vandenheuvel profited by the fact that both were veterans of the First World War, and on occasions they exchanged recollections. The roles had been reversed then. Vandenheuvel had been a prisoner of war in Germany.

To our relief, Vandenheuvel made only one change. He added to the last phrase of the preamble the words, "within existing camp rules." He also withheld, until further notice, permission to grant us any functions of self–policing. The guards were in full charge.

The Committee also made only one demand. Pleienberg insisted that the camp president remain a position appointed by the Committee. This seemed to strengthen Holländer's hand but actually the working relationship between camp and Committee was in the hands of Benedikt and Helen Pleienberg. She accompanied her husband on his camp visits but reserved her perfumed presence almost entirely for conferences with Benedikt.

"The woman drives me crazy," he fumed. "When I thanked her for what she was doing she said, 'It's fun'. I got mad. She said, 'You don't like people like me, do you'? I told her I just coudn't understand her. That she behaved like a visitor in a zoo who throws lumps of sugar to bears. She said, with that damned sphinx–like smile of hers, 'It feels good to face a bear and to know he can't do you any harm'. I told her about the bank director in Frankfurt whose sons I tutored when I was in college. Then Hitler came to power. Now the husband is dead and she is a maid in London. Guess what she said. 'This wouldn't be so uninteresting but it can't happen here'. Then I let her have it. 'That's what the woman said who is now a maid in London'. This Pleienberg snob is just plain bored."

"As long as she sends me bandages and sedatives," Berman told him. "be her bear behind bars."

"Or her lap dog," Benedikt scoffed.

7.

We held elections. Each dormitory voted for two trustees. At that time three dorms were filled, 120 men. Elected were Berman, Stein, Benedikt, Neidhart, Klingenberg, and I. The Brussels Committee sent a bagful of sheet–metal silver stars to be worn on our berets. Pleienberg, in a Napoleonic pose, took credit for this brilliant idea: in Naziland Jews were forced to wear a yellow star as a badge of shame; here the silver star was a distinction of honor. Benedikt welcomed the stars as a symbol of our community but was less enthusiastic about the gold–tinted stars Pleienberg brought for the trustees.

"We don't want class distinction in Merxplas," Benedikt objected.

But he was outvoted. The silver–star bearers needed to know whom to approach with complaints and requests. We six put on our gold stars and met in "executive session" to map out our most urgent needs. Extra food supplies. Furloughs. Visiting days for wives. A heatable room for the sick. Material for retraining.

"All right," Neidhart said, burlesquing the tone of a political speaker. "The People have spoken. The Constitution has given us departments of education, health, and labor. Every government has those. But what we need is what no other country in the world has: a department to get us the hell out of here."

8.

When I look back on my days in Merxplas I see a tumultuous conglomeration of raw–nerved men trying to scramble out of the ditch into which life had tossed them. Only when I reread my notes, the huddled masses segregate into bedraggled, grieving, angry, resigned, confused, painfully isolated individuals, tor–tured by the question of "Why me?"

In our evolution from the amoeba, memory has been a great gift. But forgetfulness is equally blissful. It would be difficult to live if the traumas and agonies of the past were not covered by the mist of oblivion. The most grievous wounds heal over, and it is not always healthy to pick at the scabs.

This was the time of the merciful lie. The truth was too painful to face. In letters to my parents I presented Merxplas as a haven and training center for my future overseas. In their letters they told me about having moved once more to a new apartment, "smaller but comfortable." The winter, thank God, was still mild. But their letters could not quite paper over the horror of a city where "uncle Camill had an accident last week," where "the Pollitzers [cousins] went on a long vacation"—a city where neighbors, and sometimes "friends," took over apartments and possessions, where the most unbelievable rumors were true, and all exit holes were plugged.

The truth had a way of seeping through.

Klingenberg received letters from his brother. The lines were widely spaced, and you could read between them when you held the paper over an oven. The truth that appeared was almost always worse than one had imagined. New arrivals brought new tales. They quickly became old tales. I became selective in writing them down.

Bruno Kostelka had found a smuggler who to take him and his sister to Luxembourg. The price was stiff because his sister had a weak leg and couldn't walk much, so they needed a car. One moonless night the smuggler's car took them toward the border. Suddenly it stopped. The smuggler pointed to a river and told them to walk from here.

The river, the Sauer, was shallow at this point. The car took off. Kostelka, a wisp of a man with narrow shoulders and spindly legs, waded in steadying his sister. The river was indeed only ankle–deep. Suddenly a clatter of motorcycles behind them. Gestapo. They turned their light beams on Kostelka. "Want to cross?" they shouted. "Go ahead." They watched the perilous wading like a stage performance. Kostelka feared a trap but he and his sister reached the other side without much trouble. Then he saw the trap. The "other side" was not Luxembourg but an island in the Sauer River. There was another arm to cross, eight meters wide and much deeper than the first. To turn back was impossible. The Gestapo was waiting. Kostelka first probed the river bed alone, to find a crossing where the water reached only up to his hip. The water was icy and he had to lean his weight heavily against the torrent. He returned to the island and crossed again, clutching his sister. "For days my jaw hurt, so tightly did I clench my teeth," he reported. "Lottie did not make a sound. We reached the other side, wet, freezing, with torn clothes. Were we really safe? I looked back. Then something strange happened. The Gestapo men stepped into the light of their beams, stood attention, saluted, hopped on their motor bikes, and roared into the darkness. They had their show and let us go. I looked at my watch to see if it was still ticking. It was. It showed ten o'clock but now we were in a different time zone. In Luxembourg it was eleven. We had lost one hour of our lives but it seemed like eternity." They found a hayloft where they hid until their clothes dried. They couldn't stay in Luxembourg and made their way to Belgium.

I remember the story well. Later that evening I asked Waniek to let me use his cubbyhole canteen and typed out a story about an English girl who was about to join her fiancé in Zürich where he worked in a hotel. They had saved her carfare and mapped their life together. On the train to Paris she met a man who swept her off her feet, as it happens in short stories. They spent two romantic days in Paris. He was an artist and urged her to go with him on an Adriatic cruise. She completely lost her head and agreed to meet him in Basle, at the train station under the big clock, at five in the afternoon. They fantasized of an exciting life together, quite different from what she had planned with her fiancé. She took the train to Basle and walked around the city, dreaming of her future. At ten to five she was under the big clock at the railroad station, feeling guilty every time the loud–speaker announced a train departing for Zürich. She watched the hand of the clock move to five, 10 after five, 20 after, and pic–tured the despair of her fiancé waiting in vain. She felt more and more like a fool, and when the loudspeaker announced a train to Zürich at 5:45 she ran to catch it. As she sat, panting, in her compartement, the lady with whom she shared it kept shaking her watch, then laughed and said, "How silly of me. I thought my watch had stopped. I just came from Paris but we are in a different time zone. My watch still shows 4:45."

9.

On November 14 a new transport arrived, with catastrophic news. Five days ago a 17–year old Jewish student, Hershel Gryn–szpan, had killed a minor official of the German Embassy in Paris. He had heard that his parents were trapped at the Polish border, after the Germans had expelled them, together with thousands, and the Polish authorities refused entry. The Nazis went on a well–orchestrated rampage of "spontaneous" rage. As I learned later, this was the pogrom that started the holocaust, the planned "final solution" of Jewry in all countries the Nazis controlled. Synagogues were burned, Jewish property smashed and looted, and some 30,000 Jews hauled to concentration camps. The new arrivals told us of beatings and arrests. A few days later letters from the survivors began to arrive, telling in circuitous ciphers of the abduction of a loved one and imploring, in even more surreptitious phrases, to find ways to help. This was still the time of murder on condition. The gas ovens had not yet been perfected. The master race still wanted to purify their country by forcing Jews out rather than exterminating them. They still released captives from concentration camps if they could leave Germany within two weeks.

These were dreadful conditions. The world was locked tight. The United States allowed immigrants with an affidavit from a sponsor and a quota number that in most cases took a year or more to mature. England admitted women who could prove they had positions as domestic help, but the visa was issued only after the position was secured. Other countries admitted immigrants who had close relatives there. I find in my notes the following list of entry conditions:

Australia: Only immigrants with capital or skills needed in the country.

Canada: Immigration practically impossible.

South African Union: Immigration practically impossible.

India: Entry granted only if re–entry in country of origin was guaranteed. (Impossible for fugitives from Hitler Germany.)

Argentina: Immigration closed October 1, 1938.

Bolivia: Only qualified agricultural workers or immigrants with £1,000. (Jews could leave Germany with only ten marks.)

Brazil: Quota system. Waiting list for years.

Uruguay: Only when re–entry to Germany is guaranteed.

Ecuador: Closed.

Haiti: Closed except for "desirable" immigrants with $5,000.

Chile: Immigration closed for one year.

Columbia: Closed until the immigration problem is solved by an international agency.

Cuba: By special permission of the ministries of foreign affairs and commerce. In addition, a capital of $500.

Kenya: Entry fee raised from £50 to £500.

Paraguay: Only qualified agricultural workers or persons with qualifications to start new industries and 1,500 gold dollars.

Peru: Limited to persons with £100 and a two-year contract by a Peruvian firm.

New Zealand: People designated as useful for the country because of special skills and capital.

It was a buyers' market, and the market was flooded with human merchandise.

10.

Every day brought letters with heartbreaking news or, worse, no letter at all. Paul Schramek became the most sought–after person. He was a large–boned, horsefaced man, with big ears and an ear-shattering voice. He had been a hawker in Vienna's amusement park, and his trumpety windpipe made him the natural choice as camp postmaster.

Mail arrived at Merxplas in late morning and was sorted alphabetically (and probably checked) in the camp office. After lunch, Schramek picked up the carton with the letters from the Administration Building, and from a bench in the dining hall called out the names of the lucky recipients. People whose name started with a low letter exchanged the news they had received, passed on rumors, voiced disappointment. It was hopeless to stop them. Only Schramek's vocal chords could outshout them.

"In emigration," Waniek observed, "an elephant's voice is worth a thousand Ph.D.s."

When the details of the big pogrom reached Merxplas, the dining room was subdued during mail handout. I was relieved because my parents had escaped the round–up. They had been evicted from our apartment and now shared two rooms with two elderly couples. Fortunately, the custodian of the apartment building had hidden them when the Jew hunters came.

Judge Stein sat next to me, clenching and unclenching his hands. When his name was called he jumped to his feet and burrowed his way through the crowd surrounding Schramek. Stein looked at the letter he was handed, and the blood drained from his face before he even opened it. We all were familiar with this kind of letter. It was sealed with the censor's band of a concentration camp.

Fred Glogau was at his side as the Judge staggered to a nearby bench. They sat, in inert desperation and Glogau, in tentative helplessness, touched the older man's hand. Stein sat, deflated, shoulders slumped, fingers drooping between his knees. Then, in a sudden thrust, Stein threw his arms around the boy and held him tight. They remained in their wretched clasp for a long time, then separated, and the Judge vacantly patted Fred's lifeless fingers. Stein's eyes met mine across the jumble of disorder, and I made my way to him.

"Fritz is in Dachau," he said haggardly. "He asks me to get him a visa. Any visa. To anywhere." He gave a rasp of a doleful laugh. "He still thinks I can fix everything. I always could."

"Get a furlough," Fred pleaded. "Go to Antwerp, see a consul."

Stein sighed deeply, staring into space, then lowered his head. "No one has yet received a furlough," he said tonelessly. "And what for? No consul hands out visas. We are sentenced, without parole."

V. A Republic Behind Bars

1.

By the end of November all four dormitories of Pavilion A were filled with 160 bewildered, indignant, noisily frustrated, and quietly desperate castoffs. But, to my astonishment, the experiment—our "playing at democracy"—began to work. The camp rules were still in force, but director Vandenheuvel made genuine efforts to incorporate our republic into his prison system. A little democracy was forming behind barred walls.

This was the daily routine one month after our first arrival:

Morning alarm at six. Lebret walked from cot to cot shaking shoulders of sleepers reluctant to wake up to reality. First order of the day: tucking in blankets according to regulations. Shivering figures hustled across the dark, misty playing field to the washroom in Pavilion B. There we took turns at rows of cold–water faucets lining a fifty–foot trough. Heinz Mautner, head of our cleaning crew, a gorilla in jeans, barked orders: "No splashing on the floor!"

("He'd make an excellent SS man," Waniek observed. Berman's comment: "Clean floors are more important than clean hands. Typical prison philosophy." The washroom was off–limits during the day, to prevent our carrying dirt from the wet washroom floor throughout the buildings.)

Next: twenty minutes of physical fitness. Martial music blared from a loudspeaker. But unlike at *Prison a Forest* we did not merely march but, on orders by Max Hutt, chairman of sports and calisthenics, we jumped, bent, stretched, twisted, and did push-ups.

7:15: breakfast bell. One hundred sixty hungry, grouchy frumps crammed into the dining hall, eight per bench, beside long tables. Two large cauldrons of black coffee were wheeled in by our kitchen crew. Recent success: the coffee was now prepared, as were all meals, by chief cook Lobositz, ex–Viennese restaurateur, and his quick-thinking volunteers. (They had realized that kitchen duty brought culinary benefits. Meals were being supplemented by shipments from Helen Pleienberg's women's auxiliary. Drawback for the kitchen crew: they had to get up earlier than the rest. Advantage: access to water three times a day. Berman used kitchen helpers to smuggle patients in need of cleaning wounds to the kitchen sink.)

Breakfast had improved. As expected of a Viennese chef, the coffee was hot and strong. Twice during that November we had the sensation of a shipment of canned milk and sugar cubes from the Brussels committee. Bread was dark and plentiful and, according to Berman, nutritious.

The next bell ordered us to the day room, where we crowded around the two iron stoves. ("Cheapest source of energy—body temperature," remarked Peter Klamm, a wiry cadaver of a man with glowing eyes and a hooked nose made more prominent by sunken cheeks. He was a chemist but had volunteered to teach auto mechanics in camp. The old car, a Steyr, had arrived at Merxplas, and no instructor was available. Klamm's qualifications: He had driven a Steyr in Austria and, as he said, "I know how to read a manual.")

Morning classes started at 8:30 (another bell). Vandenheuvel had set aside an extra building for retraining courses, plus a plot of land for would-be farmers. Spades and shovels ashoulder, a clump of men marched off into the damp morning, Koloman Gal among them. Since none of us knew anything about growing vegetables and raising chickens, a guard served as instructor. The new transports brought teachers in plumbing, tailoring, electrical work, shoe repair, carpentry, and auto mechanics.

Language classes—English and Spanish—were presented in the library room of Pavilion A. In one corner, Bruno Kostelka, a sprightly Figaro from Vienna, chattily prancing about his customers, showed his trainees how to give free shaves and haircuts. (Getting a free shave from one of the trainees was one of the minor risks in camp. Willy Kruger, our young physician and a student in the barbering class, was considered the safest because he could bandage the wounds he made.)

Morning classes ended at eleven, and we had one free hour before lunch. Max Hutt promoted soccer games during this time; he even arranged a tournament between dorms.

Lunch bell at noon. The dining hall was unheated, noisy, crowded, loaded with irritability. The soup cauldrons were wheeled in. The optimists speculated what ingenious variations of the archetypal soup-potato-cabbage menu chef Lobositz might have concocted with the help of "extras" such as dried herrings or slices of sausage.

(Benedikt hoped for "puddles of communities" to form around the tables during meal time. Some men did tend to sit together. But mostly it was grab–a–seat–while–you-can, the closer to the warm cauldron the better. As soon as the guards opened the doors, a tide of bodies flooded in, struggling for seats. The hubbub of 160 voices set 160 billion nerves on edge. Mild-mannered bookkeepers and obedient bureaucrats threw off the bridle of civilization and yielded to atavistic impulses. A popular game was "planing," a throw–back to junior–high school years: people on a bench suddenly shoved to one side so the man on the end was pushed to the floor. If he was quick and stood up at the last moment, all the others fell off.)

Horseplay couldn't hide the apprehension that built up to the moment when Schramek arrived with his carton of letters, and trumpeted out the names of the lucky (or not so lucky) recipients of mail. Reality broke the herd up into individuals with personal pains and hopes.

The next hour of free time was usually subdued, taken up with letter writing.

From 2 to 5 we returned to our classes, and the meal at 6 was a repeat of the nervous bedlam of the lunch hour. After the meal the pandemonium moved to the dayroom which our oven crew had kept heated. Franzl Jäger, our minister of entertainment, handed out packs of playing cards and chess boards. People read, wrote letters, and huddled in conversations, despite the din that reverberated from the cement ceilings, walls, and floors.

("The decibel level," said Peter Klamm, our expert in matters of technology, "is about that of a jackhammer.")

(This was the time people told me their stories, and when I wandered about with my portable in search of a quiet corner, which was increasingly difficult to find.)

In the dorms, the half hour between "lights out" and "silence" was usually filled with good–natured kidding. Perhaps the evening meal indeed contained bromides. I asked Lobositz. He said he knew nothing about it.

2.

I have repressed one painful aspect of life at Merxplas. I don't find any mention of it in my notes, although it was a cause of anguish for many and probably contributed to my developing stomach ulcers. The toilets consisted of a row of ten outhouses in the field behind Pavilion A. During the first couple of weeks I welcomed these cubby holes because they provided me with little islands of stillness and privacy where I could place my portable on my knees and type out short stories. But when the pavilion filled up, so did the ten receptacles. No water–saving device would have helped because the toilets functioned (or didn't) by gravity. I, and many others, resisted as long as we could to go anywhere near these stench holes, and Dr. Berman found psychological constipation the most widespread medical problem.

3.

The retraining courses posed a problem for me. Our Constitution stipulated that every Merxplasian had to take at least one class to prepare himself for his future life. He also had to learn a language.

Max sent me my share of the payments he received from the *Daily Herald* — a great incentive for me to turn out more short stories. I was convinced that wherever I would eventually land I would be able to make a living as a writer, an expectation grounded on little more than my futuristic optimism. I signed up in an English class, again in the optimistic hope that by the time my quota number came, I would have received an affidavit of support from an American guarantor.

These hopes were not entirely castles in the air. (I believed in castles in the air. All my shorts stories were built in cloud cuckooland, and I was convinced that before you can build even a shack on the ground you have to see it in your mind). Max was more practical. He asked the English translator of our short stories to draft an appeal for help to be sent to a dozen Epsteins, namesakes he selected from telephone directories of several American cities, and a special letter to a distant relative who had emigrated to the United States long before my birth and with whom we had no contact — in fact, I had not known she existed.

The letter that went out to namesakes was heart rending and I couldn't believe that its appeal would remain unanswered. I was sure I would establish myself as a writer in America. I needed to learn English. But retraining to be an auto mechanic or a barber I felt to be a waste of time.

I was trapped by the laws I helped to make. Everybody was to take a retraining course. No exception, lectured Judge Stein, with a schoolmaster's frown and a raised forefinger. He himself set an example by enlisting in the cobbler's class, which I considered an absurdity. He did, too, I suspected, but he signed up, partly because Fred Glogau took the class, and partly from a masochistic desire to show the senselessness of our lives. The teacher of the class was Rudi Jelinek, a hunchy little man who hoped to transfer his shoe–repair skills from the little Austrian town of Wels to the metropolis of Montevideo where he had a daughter.

I tried to bypass the retraining issue by offering a course myself, in short–story writing. This caused a good deal of hilarity but found no takers. I eventually signed up for a newly established class in artificial–flower making, mostly because I wanted to get to know the teacher better, and because few people considered artificial–flower making a promising career in Guatemala or the Belgian Congo, and the class was in danger of getting canceled.

The teacher was Kurt Berber, who had been a ballet dancer at the Vienna opera. He had a pink baby look and an eager voice that made even commonplace statements sound like fresh discoveries. Last year he had received a contract from the Teatro

Colon in Buenos Aires, which he declined. Immediately after the annexation of Austria he cabled to Buenos Aires, but the position was filled. One of Berber's Swiss students invited him to Berne, but the Swiss expelled him because Berber had entered Switzerland after an arbitrarily fixed day. He fled to Brussels. A mediocre Dutch dancing company offered him a place on their American tour. He happily signed and was to go to Amsterdam for rehearsals. But there was a frontier, and this was a pitiless block. The Dutch denied his entry despite his contract for the American tour. In desperation, Berber sneaked across the Belgian–Dutch border. After two days of rehearsals he was arrested. No intervention by the director of the dance company was of any help. Berber had broken a law by entering illegally. Eventually, after long negotiations, the Dutch consul in Brussels was authorized to grant Berber the permit to enter Holland. Although he already was in Holland, the law required that he return to Belgium to pick up the permit to enter Holland legally. The Belgian authorities granted him a one–day stay to pick up his permit, but the Dutch Consul in Brussels was suspicious and wanted to make sure that all this was on the level. This short delay sealed Berber's fate. His one–day admission lapsed and he was arrested. He protested but the Belgian authorities were used to far-fetched stories. They didn't "fall for them." In Berber's case the story was true, but before all was cleared up five days had lapsed and the Dutch company hired another dancer. Now Berber was in Merxplas and offered a course in artificial-flower making, his hobby.

I knew Berber's name from my visits to the Vienna opera, and tried to comfort him: "You'll get another break," I told him. "I'm not worried about you."

"I'm not worried about *you* either," he replied with his boyish grin. "It's just about oneself one is a bit concerned."

4.

My English teacher was Richard Berliner, the oldest man in Merxplas. He had the deep-lined face of an actor, which he had been in his youth. Most of his life, he told everyone who would listen, he had directed plays. In Berlin, Hamburg, Vienna, London. "Hamlet in London," he intoned. "Faust in Berlin, working with Reinhardt." Even Hollywood had wanted him. "And now? Pah!" He had a flair for the flamboyant, with grandiose gestures, but then suddenly he would become theatrically absorbed in his own sadness. He was the only person in Merxplas who refused to wear the camp overalls and the beret with the silver star.

"Lear, Act Five," he declaimed, with raised, nicotine–stained forefinger. "In rags, ashes in his hair, but every inch a king!"

He wore the only suit he possessed, gray, double–breasted, three–piece, custom–made, but so worn that the seat of his pants were tissue–paper thin. In one of his vest pockets he carried a monocle which he inserted into the hollow between his prominent nose and his large–circled right eye when he was about to read something.

I had never heard of him in all my theater–going years but I was fascinated, and he appreciated me as a ready audience for his blustering stories.

"You and I," he recited. "We are different. Artists! What do these philistines know of art! They lament about what they have lost. Pah! What we possess no Nazi can take away. Talent! Creativity! Imagination! We can carry them across all borders. They're in here." He tipped at his temple. "Lubitsch phoned me from Hollywood. I'm just waiting for these bureaucrats to do their paper shuffling. But first I'll go to London. Korda wants me."

Meanwhile, however, Berliner trudged around in his patent-leather shoes and furtively collected cigarette butts which he carefully emptied, using the tobacco in self–rolled cigarettes.

"I prefer to roll my own," he explained, making a ritual of lighting one of his crinkled concoctions and smoking it with the sophisticated air of the lead in a Noël Coward comedy.

He taught English for the same reason I learned flower making: to elude the demand for retraining in something "practical." He had a peculiar teaching method. Grandly he waved aside the English primers we received from Brussels as so much "crap." He monologued from Shakespeare's tragedies and staged scenes in which we had to learn the texts he had memorized. His students gradually melted away, especially when additional English courses were established. It was indeed doubtful what benefits would–be immigrants in, say, Cameron would derive from phrases such as "'Tis not for gravity to play at cherrypit with Satan." I was one of the few who stuck with Berliner while he watched the exodus of his students with bitter resignation. Shakespeare had underrated the world. Something was rotten in every country.

(The quality of Berliner's English became evident to me only years later. Early in December I received a letter in response to the appeal I had sent to namesakes in the United States. The letter came from Dave Epstein, a Hollywood banker, promising an affidavit of support and asking for some data. When I showed the letter to Berliner he became ecstatic.

"We' ll both be in Hollywood. You'll write movies. I'll direct them. We'll sweep those Yankees off their feet!"

He drafted an answer to Mr. Epstein, sending the requested data. I never heard from him. Years later, when I visited Hollywood, I called him. He said my first letter had deeply impressed him. But the second letter, from the camp, was written in such poor English that he considered me a fake.)

5.

Benedikt's hope for community began to take shape despite the simmering restlessness in the camp, or perhaps because of it. Little eddies of friendship formed in the general melee. Many jelled around the retraining courses — the "farmers," the "auto mechanics," the "cobblers." Others grew from the work forces — the kitchen gang, the oven heaters, the cleaning crew. I tended to cluster with Benedikt, Stein, and Berman. I was also drawn to the "artists," Siegfried Neumann, Franzl Jäger, Kurt Berber, and a newcomer, Hermi Schaub, a gifted young cartoonist whose tip-tilted nose sniffed out the ridiculous in our wretched situation and immortalized it in drawings that enlivened my weekly news sheet on the bulletin board. Richard Berliner deigned to play the role of benign benefactor of our low–level attempts at enter-tainment.

Then there were the staff of the "Department of Health," with their common concern to keep us fit in spite of no sickbeds, no heated room, no access to running water, only a modicum of medical supplies, and the sickening toilet situation. The core of that group was Dr. Berman, young Dr. Kruger, the ringmaster of gymnastics Max Hutt, and pharmacist Robert Klimt, a slim, long–legged stork of a man with a washboard frown that made him look perpetually irritable, which indeed he was.

Berman and Kruger shared an additional worry—a torment felt by many others: separation from their wives who lived alone in Brussels. The Krugers had left Vienna the day after their surreptitious wedding, and he had been arrested three days after arrival in Belgium.

"God still owes us a honeymoon," Kruger said. To which Berman replied, sulkily: "God isn't worshipped for his accounting methods." The Bermans had spent their honeymoon, eight years ago, in Palestine. He was a fiercely atheistic Zionist, as had been his father who named him Theodor after Herzl. Berman and his wife Karla made two attempts to reach the Holy Land, once on a decrepit Greek freighter, and again on a barge carrying wheat down the Danube to the Black Sea. Both times they were turned back by British gun boats off the coast of Palestine. Berman's scorn for the British was a close second to his hate for the Nazis. His fervent Zionism explained his puzzling outbursts against the British masters of Palestine.

Karla Berman and Susi Kruger lived by themselves in Brussels, on the Committee's weekly handout of 53 francs. Their husbands suggested that they share a room. Ostensibly to save money.

"I can't sleep thinking of Susi all alone," Kruger sighed. "She's twenty, very pretty. I can't imagine any man seeing her without wanting her."

Berman said nothing. He was a man of few words who believed in action. He made it his urgent task, as a gold–star trustee, to see that a family camp was established. Or at least that wives got visitation rights to Merxplas.

6.

An opportunity presented itself a few days later. A short notice in the Brussels daily *Le Soir* mentioned the establishment of the camp and, to my surprise, my name was mentioned. Among the inmates, it said, was "Dr. Epstein, très connu en Belgique." Actually, I was not known in Belgium to anyone but the Jewish Committee and the police. And why this well–known personality was not allowed to spend his meager British pounds on the Belgian free market, the paper did not explain. But when a young bushy–haired reporter visited the camp, he wanted to see this celebrity.

I am not proud of this episode. We had been tipped off about the visit and the camp glistened in Potemkinesk splendor. I suppose every inmate had his agenda on how he could turn this outreach to the outside world to his own advantage.

My own agenda was modest. I handed the reporter a corsage of wool–and–wire flowers made in Berber's workshop, and my latest short story. It described the ruse of a jealous husband who wished to check his wife's activities during that day by hiding her favorite pair of gloves and then "helping" her find it by retracing her suspected visits to girl friends and shops. I asked the reporter if the story could be translated and published in his paper. He carelessly stuffed the manuscript in his pocket, and I was pleasantly surprised when it was published a month later under the title, "L'Epreuve de Gant" and with the by–line "Peter Fabrizius de centre des réfugiés de Merxplas." (Peter Fabrizius was the common pen name Max and I used for our stories.)

The immediate happenings were less successful. My brief encounter with the newspaperman was broken up by Hubert Pleienberg who had brought him to the camp in his car. Pleienberg shooed me away and hustled the reporter into the library where Pleienberg planned his own impromptu press conference. He planted himself in front of the blackboard and fiddled with his mustache while he waited for the curious to squeeze themselves into the school benches. He was obviously ready for a major address.

Suddenly the door flew open and Holländer marched in like a platoon of one. He placed himself before the reporter and all but clicked invisible heels.

"I am the president of the Colony," he announced, bobbing his head in self–importance. " Sorry I'm late to greet you. I was in conference with Director Vandenheuvel. If it will please you, we can now go to my office and discuss the Colony." He loved that word. He probably saw himself as someone like the Governor of India. "I'll be glad to give you a grand tour of the camp."

Holländer had been able to wheedle a small room from Vandenheuvel, with barely enough space for a bed and a desk. Holländer no longer slept with us in the dorm. It had done wonders for his ego.

The reporter was not impressed by the invitation because he understood no German and did not know what Holländer said. Pleienberg bristled and raised himself as high as his tiptoes would allow.

"That won't be necessary," he said, with stabs of icicles in his voice. "We'll talk *here* and then *I* will show our guest around."

Holländer collapsed like a deflated bellows.

"The rat's become a mouse again," Benedikt murmured with some glee.

Pleienberg delivered his address In French. The reporter scribbled. We tried to follow Pleienberg's flowery phrases - a eulogy of Hubert Pleienberg, Belgian patriot.

The reporter was duly impressed. "Amazing. You have created here something like a little republic."

"It was a challenge to give the victims of a dictatorship the chance to hold up the banner of democracy," Pleienberg said with showy modesty.

The reporter scribbled again. "Well put. May I quote you?"

Pleienberg gracefully acquiesced. Benedikt winked at me. These were the exact words he had used to persuade Pleienberg to allow us some self–government.

Meanwhile the citizenry of the Republic had become restless in their school benches. They shouted requests in German and broken French. Pleienberg, nervously running his fingers through his sparse hair, quickly suggested, "I'll show you now the rest of the camp."

"Get us some visas," someone shouted from the back. There was a chorus of approval, orchestrated by Neidhart's "Hear, hear," and a banging on the desks in the best tradition of the British parliament.

Pleienberg did not care for British traditions. "I'll meet with the trustees later to hear their concerns," he shrilled above the clamor.

Holländer had recovered and stepped forward. "As president..." he began but Berman cut him short. His assertive voice reverberated in the turbulent room.

"What we need most is a heated space with hospital beds. Lucky we haven't had an epidemic yet."

Shouts came from all sides. Visitation rights for wives! Passes for furloughs! Better food! Tools for workshops! Family camps! And again and again: oversea visas!!

The reporter took notes, bending down to Pleienberg for translation.

So many, many needs. I felt ashamed that my request had been so banal and selfish.

VI. The Arrival of the Wolf Gang

1.

On December 4 the Wolf gang came to Merxplas.

As usually, Hubert and Helen Pleienberg arrived in their Mercedes. We had occasion for celebration. The first of our fellow inmates had received a visa and was about to leave the camp. The lucky man was Rudi Jellinek. He was to join his daughter in Montevideo. Merxplas was not a life sentence.

We gained hope, but lost our cobbler.

The Merxplas dogcatcher drove up after lunch, before the afternoon workshops began. It was a gray, drizzly day, and Max Hutt had difficulties to interest twenty–two hardy bodies in a soccer match. The rest huddled around the stoves in the day room, making space for the newcomers to line up and be inventoried. Pavilion A was filled and the new arrivals were the first to occupy a dormitory in the B Pavilion.

As always, we scanned the newcomers for acquaintances who might bring news about those we left behind.

The new arrivals filed in, carrying their suitcases, and lined up. Sommer grabbed my arm. "Look! There is Jonitai!"

The name meant nothing to me. Sommer clicked his tongue in disbelief of so much ignorance.

"A hoodlum, a crook, one of the worst. And, for heaven's sake, there is Salo Weinkraut...the whole Weinkraut mob...and there, I don't believe it, it's Heino Wolf!"

He pointed to a squat man with a crooked nose and a boldly protruding underlip. He strutted into the day room with demonstrative defiance, his battered hat on his head. Under his chin bulged a red scarf like wattles of a turkey. In Hollywood he would have been typecast with Wallace Beery.

I had learned that Sommer's scare stories needed careful checking but these characters lining up for Vandenheuvel's inspection were indeed a grubby looking bunch. Yet, even book–keepers and bank clerks looked grubby after a flight through wintry forests.

"Jewish gangsters in Vienna?" Otto Berber made a twist of disbelief. "What next?"

Sommer rolled his eyes heavenward. "You people believe all Jews are angels," he said in feigned exasperation. "The Wolf gang is a band of thieves, cutthroats, and smugglers. They made fortunes smuggling Egyptian cigarettes over the Danube from Hungary. The head of the border control was one of my customers. I *know*. From now on you better keep your suitcases locked tight."

2.

It was Benedikt's, Neidhart's and my job to inform new arrivals about the ground rules. Heino Wolf listened with faint amusement when we talked about the Constitution.

"We got the new dorm in Pavilion B," Wolf said in a voice that was at the same time hoarse and grating. "Do we get to elect our own trustees?"

Benedikt nodded miserably.

"When is the election?"

"As soon as you get to know each other."

A guffaw. "Oh, we know each other all right. How about voting tonight?"

Benedikt looked uncomfortable. "All right, tonight. You'll have two hours between dinner and bed time."

"Do we get a private room for voting?" Wolf asked. "You know, secret ballot and all that."

"You can have the library." Benedikt hesitated a moment before he said to Wolf, "You have been issued berets. No need to wear your hat."

Wolf, with a catlike grin, pushed up his hat with his thumb. "I like my lid. It's a free country, this Republic Merxplas, isn't it?"

3.

The secret ballot of the new dorm was by no means silent. There was yelling and howling behind the closed door, and from time to time something crashed against it. The four dorms in Pavilion A had elected eight trustees and we waited to see our two new colleagues.

Finally the door flew open. The new citizens of Merxplas paraded out, cheering, carrying Heino Wolf on their shoulders.

"They elected Wolf," Berman said in desperate pianissimo.

Neidhart slapped his thigh in amusement. "There was never a doubt about that. Didn't you know what crashed against the door?" He pointed at the smashed bottles on the floor.

"They brought beer from Brussels!" Klingenberg seemed dazed.

"Well," shrugged Neidhart. "It was their last chance. Waniek doesn't sell the stuff in his canteen."

Benedikt crinkled up his forehead in concern. "What now? How can we work with a fellow like Wolf?"

Wolf stepped over to us, hat on head at a rakish angle, red scarf bulging. "Well, pals," he shouted with massive satisfaction. "I'm the new elected representative. Now we'll get things done for a change! If you want something from the Committee, just tell me." He snorted in contempt. "The guys in Brussels are scared stiff of me."

We looked at one another in speechless consternation. Neid–hart saved the moment before the tension became too obvious. He crashed his callous palm on Wolf's meaty shoulder.

"Good for you," he roared. "We sure can use guys like you when the going gets tough!"

The night bell sounded. Wolf surveyed us with magnanimous contempt, touched the rim of his hat with his forefinger in a goodbye, gathered his group about him, and they marched off across the dark playing field to Pavilion B which promised to become the radical wing of our republic.

4.

The next episode in our Merxplas experiment I would not have dared to invent for one of my short stories. But life is a courageous author.

The following morning the participants of workshops gathered in the day room, to march to the building where most of the retraining classes were held. The cobbler class was leaderless, and Klingenberg, our trustee for educational matters, introduced the new teacher who was to take the place of Rudi Jellinek. Fortunately, yesterday's transport had brought a replacement, Ignaz Minkus, a hungry–looking, horse–faced, knobby man with large leathery hands. I had joined them with my notebook, to write up the new teacher for our weekly news sheet.

Minkus, chewing a toothpick, appraised the clump of men who had taken Jellinek's class.

"So you want to be cobblers?" he said with good–natured doubt. Then, with a sputter of amusement, "OK, I'll teach you all you need to know."

"Can you teach me to make the special shoes I need?" Peter Kraus asked. "That's my only pair and it's worn out."

Minkus stepped next to Kraus and lifted his clubfoot as a farrier would lift the leg of a horse he was about to shoe. Kraus, off balance, grabbed Fred Glogau's arm to steady himself.

"No problem," Minkus said, dropping Kraus's leg. "We'll make you a better one than you got now." Then his face broke into a wide grin and he held out his hand to Stein in a flush of recognition.

"Remember me, Your Honor?" he called out. He seemed gen–uinely pleased when he explained to the others: "We met once before, we two, when he sent me to the clink for three months."

There was some embarrassed laughter. Stein looked like a person in a coma. A snaggletoothed teddy bear of a man slapped Minkus on the back as if he had made a good joke. Another was busy cleaning his eye glasses. Fred looked at the judge in affectionate admiration.

"It's no big deal to have been in jail," Snaggletooth said. "Who hasn't? I in Switzerland, my brother in France." He turned to me. "And you?"

"In Brussels." I was caught off balance. I wanted to explain the obvious. That being in prison for fleeing for your life wasn't the same as burglary, or whatever Minkus had done.

"His Honor let me off easy," Minkus said cheerfully. "I was stupid to get caught."

"What did you do?" Glogau asked.

"Petty theft. Four hundred schillings. I needed the dough fast."

"To bribe a custom official," Stein said, sternly.

"You could never prove that. Now, anyway, it's water under the ol' Danube. What's the diff now? We're all in the clink and have to get out. Where you going, Your Honor?"

Stein shrugged in hopeless frustration.

"Now you know how it feels," Minkus said amiably. "That's the way the gavel bounces. What are your plans?"

"I have no plans," Stein said bleakly.

"Things will work out," Minkus said. "They always do. Well, guys, let's go to work. Where is that goddam classroom?" Klingenberg motioned toward the door and we all filed out. Minkus stayed at Stein's side. "Chances always turn up," he told him. "You just have to grab them. Paraguay, for instance. You can buy a visa for 2,000 francs."

Stein stopped in his track and stared at Minkus with a flicker of hope. Then, with a hand wave of resignation, he sighed, "Oh, these things are a fraud."

"No, no, Your Honor, this is on the level. You send the money and your passport to Rue Jardin 54, and you're in. If I had the money, you'd have to find yourselves a new teacher."

"Two thousand francs!" Glogau said. "Who has this kind of money?"

Klingenberg glanced over his shoulder and lowered his voice. "Kraus, for instance." Peter Kraus, hobbling behind us, was out of earshot. "He got it in the mail last Thursday. I stood next to him when he opened the letter."

"Perhaps he also knows about Paraguay?" Minkus ventured.

"Nay. He has his affidavit to America. Some people get all the breaks."

"We all get breaks," Minkus said, a fellow optimist. "Just don't let them slip away." He joined the others, ahead of us.

"You are not going to stay in his class?" I asked Stein.

The judge kept silent. Fred Glogau pleaded with ardent intensity: "Please?"

Stein seemed to wake up from a trance. "Why not?" he said with a shrug of hopelessness. "He served his sentence." He sipped his arm around Glogau's shoulder. "We have to serve ours."

5.

The newspaper story about the camp had done its job. The next Merxplas dogcatcher was filled with sacks and boxes of food and supplies. People were sending donations to the Committee, and Pleienberg did not miss the opportunity to take credit.

The bus arrived in the later afternoon, between dinner and bedtime. The day room was bustling with tumultuous nervous–ness. Little knots of men exchanged the latest rumors. However unbelievable, they often turned out to be less ghastly than the truth. Nightly disappearances. Foiled escapes across borders. Pleas from concentration camps. False hopes about visas. Frustrated attempts to get ship tickets.

Franzl Jäger's brother was on the "Germania." One hundred seventy refugees without visas and faced with deportation to Dachau had pooled their last resources and chartered a boat in Hamburg. The captain promised to take them to British Guiana. They weren't allowed to come even close to the shore—like carriers of the plague. They tried French Guiana. No luck. Rumor had it that Trinidad would accept them. But the captain refused to take them there unless they paid a huge extra amount. The passengers wrote desperate appeals to all who might help. Jäger was in tears.

Benedikt, in a lame attempt to comfort, said gamely, "Oh, my God. Some country will have to let them land."

Ludwig Sommer, our unfailing prophet of gloom, eagerly vol–unteered the story about the ramshackle boat, carrying a load of would–be immigrants to Palestine that sank near Crete. They would have drowned had not a ramshackle boat with a shady captain fished most of them out. "No one has heard of them again," he concluded.

"The Wandering Jew," Waniek commented. "Made in Germany. Mass produced."

"God save the King," Berman added. "For hell fire."

The trustees met in the library. Wolf and Salo Weinkraut, our newly elected colleagues from Pavilion B, sat in sardonic silence. Weinkraut, a beefy hippo, was hunched over, eyes half closed as if he feared they might give away his real thought. Wolf had his gold star attatched to his tattered hat, and looked at us with contemptuous curiosity. 'What can you do?' he seemed to ask, 'You trustees, with your gold stars?'

We talked about raising money for an emergency fund to help people like Jäger's brother, but we knew it was just talk. There were too many emergencies, and no money at all. "Some men don't have the money to pay duty for packages they received," Benedikt said. "There are mountains of such packages at the Brussels post office."

"Some don't even have the money for postage stamps," added Neidhart.

We sat quietly, each of us staring at his own kaleidoscope of fears and worries. Bernard Klein stuck his bald head through the door. "Pardon me," he said, forever apologetic.

"Come in, Klein," Benedikt said. "What is it?"

Klein was in charge of inventories, human and material. In his meticulous handwriting this prototype bookkeeper carefully entered names and data of all new arrivals in one list, and all supplies in another. He reported that a new shipment had come.

"Well?" said Benedikt. "Call your unloading crew."

Klein looked uncomfortable in his overalls too large for his dried–up limbs. "They are exceptionally heavy sacks."

"And the profs can't lift them, eh?" Wolf taunted.

"I'm afraid so," Klein said.

Wolf obviously enjoyed himself, slapping his thigh, looking at his pal Weinkraut in amusement.

"We'll get you help," Benedikt told Klein.

"Hold it." Wolf stood up, looking at us, making sure he had our attention. During the long pause I wondered what he was up to.

"I have a gold star, too," Wolf said, savoring our consternation. "That's a job for men. Come on, Salo."

The two marched to the day room and stopped at a table where his friends were playing cards. "Let's go, guys," Wolf ordered. "There's some unloading to do."

One of the players arranged his cards. "Go fuck yourself," he said routinely, without looking up. They kept on playing. Wolf stood there, quietly, waiting. Then he pounced forward and with one thrust of the hand swept the cards off the table. "Get!" he bellowed.

One of the men jumped up and faced him. Wolf grabbed him by his collar and lifted him off the ground. I had never seen anything like this except in Westerners.

The man began to choke and sputter. Wolf set him down again with a bang, and jerked his head toward the door. The man went out and the others followed. Wolf and Weinkraut went out, too. They helped with the unloading.

The rest of us gold–star bearers stood silently, looking at one another.

"It figures," said Neidhart.

6.

The trustees were kept busy. There was one emergency after another, not counting those which we couldn't do anything about—the arrests, the tortures, the killings, the suicides obliquely hinted at in letters from home. At the camp we were beset by the plugged–up toilets, the bedwetters, the night screamers, the homosexual advances, the hunger strike by the small but fanatical cluster of the orthodox who refused to eat the soup until assured it was porkless and who demanded a rabbinical determination whether the dried fish we received frequently was kosher.

There was the kitchen helper who cut off his finger and the man who needed a tooth pulled. Berman succeeded in getting emergency passes for them but the increasing number of the sick had to be kept in bed in the unheated dormitories. The medical staff had been increased by a newcomer, a veterinarian from Leoben in Austria.

"Why not?" Berman grumbled. "Who is better qualified to treat patients in pigsties?"

Then came the day when Otto Berber collapsed. Berman took his temperature and paled. He said a few words to Kruger and took off toward the administration building, off–limit territory. Guard Dierx ran after him.

Holländer, alarmed by the commotion, emerged from his office. He was no longer crouchy. He walked briskly, his whole bearing was more confident.

We told him what happened.

"Why didn't Bermann tell *me*?" he shouted, face reddening. "It's me who takes problems to *Monsieur le Directeur*. This can have dire consequences!"

"Especially when Berber dies," Kruger remarked calmly.

Holländer huffed himself up and glared at Kruger. I half expected him to say that no one was allowed to die without his permission. Berber lay horribly still. Kruger kept his fingers on his pulse.

Berman came back, with Vandenheuvel and Dierx. Vandenheuvel turned to Holländer who immediately snapped to attention. "The patient will be taken to the bed in your office. I'll order an electric heater."

"I was about to suggest this," Holländer said, bowing and walking backward like a courtier.

We carried Berber to Holländer's small room and put him to bed. Vandenheuvel was genuinely concerned. "Getting a hospital room is difficult," he explained to Berman. "It requires structural changes and permission from the authorities. It took us a year to get one for the homeless."

"Couldn't we use theirs?" Berman suggested.

"*Je suis désolé.*" I knew that phrase. It was the most definite 'no' Belgian bureaucrats could utter. "Our contract says, no mingling with the homeless."

"Arent we homeless enough?" Berman muttered, more to himself. Then, to Vandenheuvel, with acid irony: "Perhaps some day the authorities will allow us to share their cemetery."

7.

The crisis had a positive result. At least, I thought so.

The next day Holländer strutted into the library where we trustess met and announced that he had succeeded in wrangling a concession from Vandenheuvel. We were allowed to police our own affairs. The guards would be on the premises but take action only when things got out of hand.

Benedikt's eyes widened in pleasure. "That's a real step toward independence. Tell the *directeur* we appreciate it."

I thought Vandenheuvel felt guilty about his inability to get us a sick room, and wanted to make things up.

Benedikt radiated excitement. "Self–policing means more than waking up the men in the morning and ringing the dinner bell instead of the guards doing it. We'll have to show that we can run our lives in camp."

"Within the Constitution," Stein cautioned. "It stipulates our right to discipline ourselves."

"This means," Klingenberg intoned, "we have to assume responsibility for our behavior."

"It means not a goddamned thing," Weinkraut said. "The guards are still in charge."

"It will depend on how well we do it ourselves."

"It means," Neidhart said in a no–nonsense voice, "that we'll have our own police force and someone running it."

Holländer indicated he was available. Which caused Wolf to break out into a horse laugh.

"Holländer," Benedikt said diplomatically, "you have enough on your hands. We'll have to think about this."

"Submit your proposals to me," Holländer sniffed and stalked out of the room.

"Just imagine," Wolf grinned. "That bubble-headed nincompoop as chief of police!"

"Happens in the best countries," said Neidhart.

8.

With Berber sick, there was no flower class. I went to see him twice a day and sat at his bed. His fever was down, but so was his spirit. Berber, the irrevocable optimist, was depressed. For the first time he really worried about his future. He felt weak, and his weakness made him doubt if he would ever be able to dance again. He told me that his suitcase contained only one suit but five costumes, his greatest treasure. I listened to the stories about his childhood in a middle–class Viennese home of assimilated Jews similar to my own. They went to the synagogue only on the high holidays, more to please his grandfather than from religious convictions. He fasted on Yom Kippur but always cheated a little. The family held the Seder ceremony in grandpa Samuel's home, to praise God for the exodus. But why praise God for leading the Israelites out of slavery, and not blame Him for letting them become slaves?

"Do you believe in God?" Berber asked.

I had asked myself that question many times during the past year. And I truthfully said that I didn't know.

But he didn't listen to me. He no longer talked about God, he talked *to* God. In whom he probably did not believe.

"Why do you do this to us?" he whispered. "Do you really want to do it, or did you make a mistake? What's your purpose? To test us? Punish us? Cleanse us? Prepare us for another life? Make us feel your power, get us to bring you sacrifices, give you gifts? What gifts can we bring to a God who has everything? We need a miracle. Oh, how we need a miracle!"

He groaned. I got up to call Berman but Berber held my sleeve. "Don't go," he pleaded. "Get me a pencil and a paper."

"What do you want to write?" I asked.

"A poem," he said, his eyes glistening. "My grandfather always told us: if you feel pain write a poem. It will help others in pain."

Exhausted, he fell asleep.

9.

Twelve o'clock sharp the lunch bell sounded, still rung by guard Lebret. The men, having returned from their courses, hungrily massed in front of the dining hall door, and when it opened, poured in like lava. They struggled for seats near the center of the room where the soup cauldrons would stand so they would be first to be served by the kitchen crew. Tables and benches had been added for the residents from Pavilion B until a second dining hall could be opened there. The room was more crowded and noisier than ever.

To me, these turbulent moments in the dining hall were the most trying. A fiery ball was forming in my stomach. That day the food was late and the men, especially the young, banged their spoons on the table and shouted in chorus:

"We - want - our - food!"

The guards stood by, nervously, in pairs.

Waniek, pale, with almost colorless eyes, stared sadly at where, in his former, orderly life, the crease would have been in his pants. "Listen to them. They sound like the mob shouting, 'We - want - our - *Führer*!' Frightening how the Nazi witchery works even on our youngsters. What can we expect of the Germans?"

Stein, next to me, spoke so faintly I could hardly hear him. "A doomed generation. Contaminated from childhood. They'll be lost even after this spook is over."

The soup cauldrons were wheeled in. The crowd booed. Lobositz who ordinarily choreographed his crew with the grace of a headwaiter, bristled. He bristled easily. As he glared at the hostile crowd, the booing increased. He finally lifted the lid from the cauldrons and his helpers ladled out the soup. Then he opened a barrel and distributed today's extras: dried herring.

Somebody smacked his herring against the wall. Others followed.

"Every day these goddamned herrings!" a red–faced heavy–weight bellowed, his eyes popping.

"Three weeks ago we would have been glad to have them," Max Hutt shouted into the hubbub.

"The store room is full of food," Jonatai roared. "We unloaded it. Where is it? Probably in the bellies of Holländer and his gold–star brass."

"Let's get it!"

A volcano of rage erupted. The voices of sanity were drowned out by a fury of desperation. Klein, the keeper of the store room was rushed and in terror surrendered the keys. In the general melee Neidhart who threw himself against the crowd was knocked down. Max Hutt and his athletic crowd were swept aside. We saw Dierx running for help, blowing his whistle.

"Here goes our independence," Benedikt said sadly.

Wolf pushed his hat up his forehead. "You are all a bunch of shitheads," he said in a voice heavy with contempt. He forced his way through the mass of bodies and snatched the keys from the heavyweight who was about to leave the hall. When the man resisted he received a chin hook that sent him reeling against the men behind him. Two huskies who attacked Wolf received knock-out blows. The man exuded pure animal energy. The crowd froze.

"Don't be silly, pals," Wolf said in his husky, low-pitched voice. "Sit down and eat."

"Get us some decent food," someone shouted. Others joined in. Wolf commanded silence with one sweep of his hand. "I am your trustee," he said, "and I'll get you some decent food. Just keep quiet."

Everybody scampered back to his seat. Wolf commandeered Weinkraut and Jonatai to come with him.

Holländer appeared from his private room. He shrank back when he faced Wolf. "What happened?"

"You got to get them some extras, pal," Wolf said. "Sausage or cheese."

"What do you mean, I got to?" Holländer flared up.

Wolf moved close and squinted at him. Wolf's hard bright eyes were like chips of quartz. Then he broke into a grin. A threaten–ing grin. His fists were clenched.

Holländer began to babble. "If you think...tell Klein... "

"I got the keys and two men to carry the food. There was a bit of trouble. They're calling the boss."

"Trouble?" Holländer slapped a hand before his mouth. "And no one told me?"

"I'm telling you now, buddy." Wolf grinned broadly. "Every–thing's okay. Don't you worry. We'll get some extras. Do we have salami?"

"Yes but..."

"No buts. I'm a trustee, see?" He pointed at the gold star on his hat. "You straighten things out with the big man, okay?"

He left with Weinkraut and Jonatai just about when Vanden–heuvel arrived with six guards. The dining hall was quiet.

"I've taken care of things," Holländer reported.

"Good," Vandenheuvel said. "It sounded serious."

"It was serious," Holländer acknowledged. "I ordered salami to be handed out."

Vandenheuval nodded in approval. "You handled it well."

Wolf and his two friends came back with three sacks and handed Klein the keys.

Klein later checked the store room. Nothing was missing but the sacks with salami.

10.

Neidhart said it first.

We were on our way to the library to meet the other trustees.

"Wolf would make a good police chief."

The thought had been on the fringe of my mind, too, but I had dismissed it. To appoint a gangster chief of police was an ingenious surprise twist for a story but crazy in real life.

To my amazement, Benedikt said, "I thought about it, too."

I looked at Judge Stein. He was strangely quiet. Maybe he had thought about it, too. Maybe we had all thought about it.

Neidhart put it in words. He pointed at the black and blue mark under his right eye. "Wolf's the only one who can handle that mob."

Klingenberg said, in a small voice, "A breakdown of values. The age of the club–law. Government by violence. Are we going to join it?"

"Let's face it," Neidhart said. "Our choice is the guards or Wolf."

"Choosing the lesser evil," Klingenberg said, sadly. "The downfall of democracy."

"What do you think, Stein?" asked Benedikt.

The judge withdrew into his own thoughts. A jury of one. And came up with a verdict.

"We live in a new age. I despise it but we have to face reality."

"You think it will work?" I asked.

"No," said Stein. "But nothing else will, either. If we give him some responsible assistants we may get some kind of order."

Wolf and the other trustees were in the library. Our main business of today was to implement Vandenheuvel's permission to police ourselves.

"How can we handle this?" Benedikt looked around the circle. "It's still a prison, with guards and everything. But we did not do badly this noon."

"Thanks to you, Wolf," Neidhart addressed Wolf directly. "That's why you'd make an efficient head of our self–policing."

Wolf looked at him, round–eyed like an owl.

"It would be your responsibility to keep order in the camp," said Benedikt.

"You can do it, Wolf," Neidhart added. "Perhaps only you."

Wolf seemed frozen. Only his owl eyes blinked.

Weinkraut's bulk doubled up with mirth. "Heino—head of police?"

"Shut up, Salo," Wolf said, sternly.

"You accept the nomination?" Stein asked, following protocol.

"Sure," Wolf said, fully in control of himself again.

"Any other nominations?"

Wolf looked around, his wattles–scarf bulging. No one uttered a sound.

I felt scared myself.

"Nominations are closed," Stein announced. "All in favor of making Heino Wolf head of our security department?"

The ayes were a bit thin but unanimous.

"Pals," Wolf said, "I thank you. I'll get things done for you."

We looked at one another in consternation. Had we just doomed our experiment?

VII. Women at Merxplas

1.

The Jewish Committee in Brussels made us a Chanuka present.

Pleienberg announced it after Schramek's trumpet voice silenced the cacophony in the dayroom.

"I am happy to tell you," Pleienberg began importantly but stopped when his voice became squeaky. After he took a deep breath, he continued in sonorous dignity: "I am happy to tell you that I was able to persuade the Security Office of the Belgian government to grant, from time to time, visiting rights to the wives of the detainees."

In the explosion of cheers, I noticed a flicker of mockery on Helen Pleienberg's lips. Probably her husband was once more taking credit for something *she* had accomplished.

The great day was to be the next Sunday, December 18.

But, to reverse the famous fortune-cookie wisdom, every opportunity has its crisis.

Wednesday, after lunch, Peter Kraus limped up to me and, with a conspiratory wink, asked me to follow him outside. He went to the far end of the soccer field, within the stench of the wretched toilets. It was a miserable, drizzly day. A lifeless gray sky smothered the world. Kraus wore a heavy overcoat, face behind the up-turned collar, hands jammed deep into the pockets. His reptilian eyes darted back and forth, although no one was within earshot. His voice was barely audible.

"There's going to be trouble."

"What kind of trouble?"

"Serious trouble." He took out a cigarette and lit it with shaking hands. "I don't know who to tell."

I was used to such confidentiality, and found it best not to prompt.

"I'm in the cobbler class," Kraus began.

"I know."

"Minkus is the teacher."

"I know," I repeated.

"This morning, in class, Minkus took me aside, and asked me . . ." He was unable to continue, took a deep drag on his cigarette, and had a spasm of coughing. Then he grabbed my sleeve and pulled me down until my ear was at the level of his mouth, and said quickly: "He asked me if I wanted a piece of ass."

I didn't comprehend. I had expected something horrible, and was so relieved I almost laughed, but his expression of fear stopped me.

"Don't you understand?" he whispered. "Minkus — the gang — will bring whores out here, pretending to be their wives. It's a business. 100 francs a shot."

My first reaction was still relief — this was the stuff short stories were made of. But I realized the consequences if Vandenheuvel learned of it.

"I'm glad you told me," I assured Kraus. He was visibly shaking.

"Don't tell anyone I told you," he whimpered. "They'd kill me."

Benedikt and Stein were playing chess in a corner of the day room. Neidhart was kibitzing. I told them.

"Good Lord, what next?" Benedikt put his elbows on the table and rubbed his face with his palms. "What can we do?"

Stein massaged the bridge of his nose. 'We can't tell Vandenheuvel. No point in telling Holländer. And our chief of police is the gang leader."

I couldn't resist. "A wolf in sheeps clothes," I said.

Neidhart smacked his right fist against his left palm. "That's it," he called out. "We'll tell Wolf."

We looked at him in consternation.

"He may not be in on this," Neidhart explained. "And even if he is he'll call the deal off if we tell him he's the only one who can save us. Let me handle this, okay?"

"We're getting deeper and deeper into a morass." Stein sat hunched over, lost. "We use pimps to stamp out prostitution."

"It takes one to know one," Neidhart said. He stood up, and waited for a fraction of a second, but neither of us stopped him. His gold tooth gleamed as he left.

Just when the bell announced the beginning of afternoon classes, Neidhart came back. His thumb and his forefinger formed a circle which he kissed in a gesture of triumph, as he disappeared in the jostling crowd.

"It takes one to know one," Benedikt quoted.

2.

Today, when I leaf through the album of my mental pictures, that Sunday stands out. My notes recall the "facts" but the moods and meanings have become clearer in retrospect.

It was a rare, sunny December day. Dotted puffy clouds floated in the washed blue sky, the air smelled of spring.

Not really. The sky was rinsed but the smell of spring was in my imagination. The air *should* have smelled of spring. It actually smelled of shoe polish.

For the first time since our arrival, most of us wore street suits, often the only ones we possessed. We shaved, even those who didn't expect a visitor, like myself. Ordinarily we looked forever unshaved, despite Kostelka's barbering class. And we waxed our shoes. Shoe polish was in hot demand, and Waniek's supply was hopelessly sold out.

The first to arrive was Lucille Clairmont. She drove her father's tractor from near-by Turnhout. She parked by the side of the road that led to the Administration Building which was off limits for us. Koloman Gal must have been in contact with her. He was right at the hedge bordering the road — as far as we were allowed to go. They ran into each other's arms and kissed. I felt like applauding. What a curtain raiser!

The Merxplas dogcatcher came at about eleven. Those who expected or hoped for visitors, had been massing along the hedge for an hour and broke into cheers as the van passed by on its way to the Administration Building for the check-in. They craned their necks to see if their visitor was among the arrivals. I fervently hoped that nothing would go wrong. Could Minkus and his pals have smuggled in their girl friends? Neidhart had assured me that Wolf had promised to take care of the problem. Still, my stomach clenched, as it did irritatingly often.

The checking over, the women sprinted toward the hedge and into the arms of the waiting men. Some lifted their women high into the air, others hugged them quietly. Many of the men looked blank. "She didn't have the money," Max Hutt said, lips pressed to thinness in disappointment. "Fifteen francs — we used to spend more on movie tickets."

Most of the women were young, almost children, quickly married before emigrating into the unknown. Their parents, families, friends left behind, they had no one except each other. They clung to each other as to mutual life belts. In normal circumstances, most would not have married; the basis for marrying was shared insecurity. Outward possessions — money, positions, careers — were lost. What counted were inner qualities, or sometimes illusions of inner qualities: reliability, commitment, belief in each other.

All this is clearer to me now than it was then. What cheered me that December morning fifty years ago was the bubbling laughter, the fruity smell of women, the glittering dresses, the spots of color that brightened the grayness of the cement barracks. The hubbub in the day room was as strident as ever, but it contained a splash of gaiety. Here was hope — and proof — that the movie of life was not entirely in black and white.

Waniek seemed to have similar thoughts but a more pessimistic bent. "Women bring out the true nature in men," I remember him saying. "I never noticed what a handsome dog Schramek is. And what a flabby scarecrow Klingenberg, with all his professorship. Without women we men are an undistinguishable mass of unshaven clowns. Only the fair sex brings out our true personality. A disgraceful discovery."

I felt shy intruding on the privacy of the couples but Berman and Kruger came up to me and introduced their wives. Karla Berman was a black-haired beauty with a serpentine body, enormous charcoal eyes, and a generous mouth. Susi Kruger was a wispy girl, with light skin and barely visible freckles, sapphire blue eyes wide open and glittering with excitement. The two were a study in contrasts: Karla well-groomed, self-assured; Susi, her hair slightly tangled, careless, vulnerable, soft, defenseless. They had followed the advice of their husbands and taken a room together, to save money and relieve their loneliness.

"An attic," Karla reported. "But comfortable. We cook our soup on the gas heater, cover the cracks in the furniture with pretty scarves, and pin photos on the bare walls."

"You Clark Gable, and Susi her husband," Berman laughed.

"We've cut out the picture of an elegant dining room from an illustrated," Susi said in her little girl's voice. "In front of that we eat our sardine sandwiches."

Kruger put his arm around Susi's waist and pulled her close. "You probably would find a way to make Merxplas pretty. "With scarves and photos."

"Men have no imagination," Karla remarked. "These barracks are hideous."

"Still," said Susi, "I'd rather be here with Willy than alone in Brussels. It's awful there, too. The men don't know what to do with themselves. They pace back and forth like in a cage, the older ones suffer most. Many live in slums, four or five in a room."

"I hate that poor-people milieu." Karla shook her head in disgust, her long hair swinging. "It's a morass. One step and you're lost. I try to get acquainted with the Belgian women at the Committee. I met a delightful lady, a volunteer. Madame Pluvier."

Berman's interest was aroused. "Is her husband Louis Pluvier?"

"That's her son. You know him?"

"Pleienberg mentioned him. He donated some medical supplies, such as they are. He has money and influence. I hope he'll get us a sick room."

"His mother is in the women's auxiliary."

"Karla," Berman said with great intensity, "could you talk to his mother about more help?"

"Is it so important?"

"A matter of life and death, truly. Without a minimum of medical equipment I can't keep on working." He glanced at his wrist watch. "Excuse me a moment. Berber's temperature went up again this morning."

The last sentence was addressed to Kruger who didn't listen. He and Susi were lost to the world. Karla was left alone. She looked at me, quizzically, and gave a nervous little toss of her cascading black hair.

"You are a writer?" she asked.

"Trying to," I said.

"What do you write?"

"Oh, nothing much. Little love stories."

She stared at me with an expression of curiosity that made me uncomfortable.

"Will you read one to me?" Her voice was rich, throaty. I hadn't heard a woman's voice in almost two months. I looked away. Willy Kruger and his wife were deeply entangled in a kiss. I felt trapped and I liked it. And didn't like that I liked it. The heroes in my stories would know what to do.

I was saved by the bell calling us to the dining room. The rush to the door got under way, but slowed. Ladies first. The veneer of civilization was still in place.

3.

Benedikt must have told Natascha about the Minkus scheme. "There was a buxomy type paying the bus fare at the Committee," Natascha said. "With a pale, frightened looking kid still in her teens. Nobody knew them. They weren't on the bus, though."

"Wolf nixed them," Neidhart nodded. He sat with us at the "women's" table — Natascha, Karla, and Susi with their husbands, Stein, Glogau, Klingenberg, and I.

"A mother-daughter streetwalker team?" Klingenberg twirled the gray beard that covered his wattles and jowls making him look like an Old-Testament prophet.

"Why not?" Natascha looked at him with flickering eyes. "I've seen in Russia what women will sell to survive, if they have nothing else to sell."

"Marxist immorality," Klingenberg mumbled.

"These were society women," Natascha told him harshly. "Fleeing from the Marxists."

"A breakdown of values." This was Judge Stein's favorite phrase which he often uttered with a bland face of utter hopelessness. He disliked disorderliness and suffered from his impotence to dispense order.

"Outdated values," Neidhart said. "Making room for new ones."

"Values are eternal," Klingenberg lectured.

"Chicken values," Neidhart said gruffly. He told about fleeing with some friends from the Nazis in 1935. Nearly starving, they found a chicken farm where they dug a hole, put in it some grains of wheat, and trapped it with a loop of rope. Then they hid in a bush. "Soon they came, six, seven chicks. One sticks its head into the hole, wham! Got him. They others scramble off, scared. After a while they come again. Another one sticks its head into the loop. Wham. So it went with them all."

"Stupid birds," Karla laughed.

"No more stupid than people. They kept sticking their heads into the hole Hitler dug for them. First in Germany, then Austria, now Sudetenland. No one learned from the others."

"What's your point?" asked Stein.

"We need a new way of thinking. Away from the me-me-me to the we-we-we. Look at the people here in the camp. Six hundred me-me-mes. Every man for himself, and so all go down."

"And you?" Stein challenged him. "Are you not out for yourself?"

"You bet," Neidhart grinned. "If a guy works for others, and the others only for themselves, he's not a man of the future. He's a fool."

4.

As a special treat, Vandenheuvel permitted us to walk through the heath beyond the hedge. But only in groups of ten or more.

"So nothing immoral will happen," Karla said with a flicker of mockery.

"When I was engaged to Teddy, I was barely eighteen, and my mother let me visit him only in daylight. She thought sex only could happen after dark."

"And she was right," Bermann said in his deep rumble.

"Because we were fools," Karla remarked with unexpected vehemence. "Living by outdated chicken values." She turned to me. "You're a writer. Your name was in the paper. Do you write about the new values? What are they?"

I was not prepared for this direct attack. Karla challenged me with her smoldering eyes. The wind had whipped color into her cheeks, her mouth was inviting, her eyes so alive! She had thrown off her overcoat, and the flesh of her arms and shoulders showed through the loosely woven fabric of her dress. Berman had walked on with Stein and Klingenberg. I was alone with Karla and badly wanted to impress her, say something profound, but nothing came to mind. I grabbed her hand and kissed it, hungrily, in wretched loneliness. Her hand smelled fruity, I turned it over and kissed her fingers, licked her palm. It was a moment of madness; I am not proud of it. She was adrift, needing an anchor, and I didn't help. She gasped with pleasure and our eyes locked. There was a force in her, bursting to spring free that delighted and scared me. I let go of her hand.

Gal, Lucille, Benedikt and Natasha came by. I'll never know how much they saw and guessed. Natasha grabbed Benedikt's and my arm and we ran into the heather.

"No straying from the path," Gal called out, mimicking the policeman. "Vandenheuvel's orders!"

"Who's got the gold star?" Natasha plopped down and pulled us with her. "You or my Koby?" She looked around, her eyes dancing. "It's beautiful. So many rabbit holes. In spring I'd like to come out here and paint."

"In spring I'd like to be in Australia," Benedikt laughed. "There you've got even more rabbit holes."

"You paint?" I asked her.

"I dabble in it," she admitted, but Benedikt added, "She is a great portrait painter. In Frankfurt we called her the Russian Klimt."

They got lost in recollections. "You didn't think of marrying me in Frankfurt, did you?" she asked.

"I often wondered. We clicked but there was something strange between us. That's fallen away."

"The emigration." Natasha was lying on her stomach, propping up her chin and staring into the distance. "When I told you about our flight from Russia, across frozen lakes, wolves howling, you didn't believe me. No one believed us. You saw me as what you wanted to see me — a doll, not a woman. You looked at me with amused eyes and thought these were made-up stories. I didn't have to make up any stories. You know that now. You have gone through emigration yourself. Emigration is painful, and pain makes you grow. When you saw me paint, you were amazed. I was amazed myself. The pain made me a better artist, a more understanding person. I would not want to go through that anguish again, but in some moments I am grateful for it. Sometimes I think God loves people more whom he sends suffering. You'll say that's too 'Russian', too 'Dostoevski', but that's how I see it."

Karla, Lucille, and Gal had joined us. Two pairs, Karla and I. The heather exhaled its delicious sugared breath. Benedikt tenderly kissed Natasha's eyelids. "I often thought of you, Pixy," he said, calling her by a name that must have been their secret, but he had forgotten our presence. "I remembered your stories when I carried you through the river. When we sat in the dark forest and it started to snow. When I left our room at five in the morning to escape police raids. I asked myself, 'is this really happening to me? That I walk in a prison court with jail birds? That I share a vagrant camp with professors and bank directors?' I know now what I didn't understand then: that you are a doll and an artist at the same time."

We sat quietly. The orange globe of the winter sun hung low in the hazy sky. Lucille, her legs folded under her, looked at Gal. "You are an artist, too."

He shook his head. 'That's over." There was great sadness in his voice.

She took his hand and plucked at his fingers, one at a time. "Want to tell me?"

"A simple story. Happens every day. But it's different if it happens to *you*." He took a deep breath. "We were three on a flying trapeze, two men and a woman. We all had the skills, but the ideas were mine. We were performing in Vienna when the Nazis marched in. I'm half Jewish, the two others are 'Aryans', he was an illegal Austrian Nazi. He denounced me, saying I had had an affair with our partner. Racial rape, the new crime. I fled. A month ago I received rave reviews about 'our' trio. They were performing in Berlin. They had replaced me with a new pure-blooded Aryan . The papers praised their imaginative routines, which I had thought up and tried out all by myself."

Lucille avoided his eyes, asking the grassy ground: "And . . . was he right . . . about the affair?"

"We were engaged to be married," Gal said softly.

"And now?"

"Now she's married to the other one."

Lucille smoothed down her peasant dress. "And you will look for new partners?"

He gave a nervous toss of his long blond hair. "No. My hands are no longer steady enough. I'll become a farmer in Bolivia, or in some other godforsaken place."

I watched Karla during these talks. She sat erect, nibbling on a stalk of grass. Now she spit out the grass and exploded, "The whole world is in shambles. We live by new rules."

The two couples were caught up in their own worlds. I felt alone with Karla but she paid no attention to me. She sat still, only her earrings quivered in the breeze. She sat, with pouty lips, twisting her wedding ring.

5.

When our little group came back from the walk, the dayroom radiated activity, swirling around the brightly colored flecks of womanhood in the mass of jostling, drab men.

"I'll have a look at my patients," Berman told Karla. "They are in their beds in the unheated dorm. It's a disgrace."

"And I'll show you my castle," Benedikt bowed to Natascha. "The seventh cot from the door."

But the stairs leading to the second floor were blocked by Dierx. "The dorms are off limit," he snapped. He let Berman pass but not the rest of us.

"Something's happened," Benedikt said. "Let's go see Holländer."

In his cubbyhole, Holländer paced back and forth, his face as red as the horseshoe of his hair. In front of him stood Kruger and Susi. She seemed more frail and vulnerable than ever.

"They were caught kissing in the dorm," Holländer stormed. "On a bed! Lying down!"

"I can't bring myself to being terribly shocked," Natascha remarked.

"Heavens!" Kruger called out. "It's no crime to kiss your wife when you have been married for three months and haven't seen her in three weeks!"

"I can understand it," Holländer said sharply, "but not permit it. I am responsible for the camp. The incident has been reported to the director. What happens if the visits are banned again?"

"I'll see what I can do," Benedikt promised.

Holländer erupted. "You? Who are *you*? I'll have to straighten things out! Always I!"

A large, lumpish woman, who quietly sat on the cot, put her fleshy hand on his arm. "Please, Ernst. Your heart. Don't get excited."

"I don't really understand your excitement," Benedikt said, but Holländer shouted him down.

"You don't understand anything! None of you! You think you trustees can fix things! I am the president, no one else! You are nothing if I don't cover you!"

Benedikt saluted with exaggerated exactness. "Yes, *mein Führer!* " He turned and marched out in goose steps. Outside he broke into a laugh.

"The little man who gets swept to power — where have I seen this before? This time it's not Hindenburg and Krupp, it's Vandenheuvel and the Committee. They picked Holländer because they can control him. So they let him have power. The joke is that he believes it. He was Mister Nobody in our first transport, and now he has his own room and orders people around."

"I sat next to his wife in the bus," Natascha reported. "She never stopped gabbing, told me her whole life story. And his. I got the impression she had him on a leash. 'I can't see Ernst in charge of a camp,' she cackled. "He couldn't even handle the kids. Once he was secretary of a bowling club and made a mess of it.' She couldn't wait to see how he handled himself."

Well, now she knew. She had been sitting in the corner, startled and shaky. He had succeeded in impressing her with his authoritarian arrogance, making a glorious display of being the man of destiny.

Our destiny.

6.

When Berman returned from his medical round, Kruger immediately rushed to him. Kruger spoke to him with great intensity, and I saw with alarm that Berman paled. The corners of his mouth drooped. Susi stood alone, crushed, with red-rimmed eyes.

She startled when I put my hand on her arm, and she made a brave attempt at forcing a smile

"Oh, come on, Susi," I tried. "This thing'll blow over."

A single tear rolled down from the corner of her eye. Then she threw herself against me, buried her face on my shoulder, and sobbed. Nobody in this mad, whirling crowd paid attention to us. Hugging couples were everyhere.

After a long while she lifted her head and wiped her eyes with a handkerchief. "He won't let me have it." Again she burst into tears, crumpling her handkerchief up into a ball.

"Let you have what?"

She made several attempts at speaking, then took my hand and placed it on her stomach. My first reaction was relief. In our family there had always been great joy when a woman became pregnant. But it immediately hit me that times had changed.

"Karla envies me," Susi said. "They've tried for years." Then, with a ferocity for which I was unprepared, her tiny fists pummeled my chest. "I've lost my home, my parents, my friends. I want something that 's mine!"

I could think of dozens of reasons why Kruger was right under the circumstances, and I also knew that Bermann would find a "reasonable" way to snuff out this emerging life. The world was indeed in shambles. The old rules were smashed. What used to be a blessing was now a tragedy. I held Susi's waiflike body and thought of Karla.

7.

At dinner, Karla sat opposite me, across the table. She seemed vibrant, agitated, paid no attention to the haze of small talk at our table, and even less to the hubbub in the rest of the dining hall. The tip of her tongue slipped out like a lizard's and darted in and out between her small white teeth and her wet lips. I found it difficult to keep my eyes off her and was hoping my attention wasn't noticed. Benedikt and Natasha had only eyes for each other, Kruger and Susi whispered busily, their heads only inches apart. Her expressionless eyes made me suspect that he was convincing her to do the "reasonable." Stein and Klingenberg were off on some philosophical extravaganza.

"Karla," said Berman. "You won't forget about Madame Pluvier."

She fiddled around with her spoon. "No," she said. "I won't. About the medical supplies."

"And the sick room."

"The sick room," she repeated.

"Heated."

"Oh yes, heated."

I felt her knee touch mine under the table. I shifted my legs but she kept shifting hers. During the rest of the meal our entire calves were in contact while she kept up her conversations with whoever spoke to her. Once or twice her febril eyes looked at me with a directness which, in spite of myself, I liked.

8.

After the meal we crowded into the dayroom where the benches were arranged in rows like a theatre. A few tables, joined, formed the stage. The first rows were reserved for the visitors and their husbands. This arrangement kept me from the Bermans, which saddened and relieved me.

Franzl Jäger was the master of ceremonies. He chattered as nonchalantly as during our nightly kidding before lights-out. Neumann had arranged a program including singers, poetry readers, an accordion player, a magician, and one of his own skits. The performance barely ended before the bed-time bell, so the time for saying goodbye was mercifully brief. I saw Karla from the distance while the women entered the Merxplas dogcatcher. She gave me a smile and a flutter of her fingers.

9.

I could not fall asleep for a long time. So much had happened in that one day! When I look now at my notes, I see a jumble of infantile philosophy, wishful thinking, confusion, but also the seeds of new growth. Yes, the world was in shambles, much of what we had treasured worthless, our lives built on quicksand. And yet, I detect in my notes an awareness of firm ground for a new foundation. They contain experiences confirming my optimistic conviction that the sun shines even behind the darkest clouds, and that the morality of Snow White has validity in real life. I can read into these old scribbles my first realization of what proved to be a life saver: that, to survive, I must learn to rely on my inner resources regardless of outer circumstances.

Perhaps I read too much into these old notes. What I remember are hours of doubt and despair, not with matters of philosophy, but with the very real conflict of being so strongly attracted to the wife of one of my best friends in the camp. My morals were safe behind the walls of Merxplas, but what would I do if I had a day in Brussels? Could I withstand the physical lure of those inviting eyes, that throaty voice?

My fantasies formed into a story I called "Seduction." A young man in London (let's call him Joe) is asked by his friend in Brighton (let's call him Theodor) to show the sights of London to his visiting wife. For three days Joe drives the charming woman (let's call her Karla) around the city, to parks, museums, historical landmarks. They go to the theatre, eat in restaurants. Joe is attracted to Karla but is careful to make no advances, not because he has scruples, but because he is afraid she might reject him and tell her husband. On the last evening of her visit he drives her back to her hotel and takes an unusual route. After a few minutes of silent driving he takes out a key and holds it in his hand. Karla looks at him with suspicion. "What key is this?" she asks. He drives on, without a word. "Where are you driving me?" No answer. "What are you planning to do?" Her questions become more and more intense. Without his response, her words are an anxious, pleading, cajoling monologue. "We had wonderful three days together, but what right do you have to take me to your apartment? . . . I know you find me attractive, and I like you too, but please don't assume that gives you the right to have an affair with me. I love Teddy, would not want to hurt him. Please don't look so down-hearted, I don't want to hurt you either." (And so on, fill in the details. Finally): "All right, just this once, but swear that Teddy will never know." At that, Joe makes a U-turn and drives to his apartment.

Having shifted my problem to a fictional level, I fell asleep.

VIII. Justice 1939

I.

The next stretch on the Merxplas rollercoaster was a steep dip.

The day after the women's visit started with routines but ended in a shocker. After the evening meal, Schramek trumpeted a call to order in the fermenting dining room. Neidhart stepped on a table; his jaw was locked in a tight clinch. I noticed that eight guards lined the walls.

"Comrades," Neidhart intoned gravely, "for the first time in our life together one of us has committed a common crime. Someone has stolen 2,000 francs from comrade Kraus. The thief cannot escape. We know the serial numbers of the banknotes. We'll find him and punish him severely. He'll be shipped back to Germany. But there's one more chance. Check your pockets. The person who finds the money, will get a finder's reward..."

Kraus, his eyes squinched with anguish, struggled furiously to his feet and angrily jerked forward. Neidhart swept away his protest. "A finder's reward," he repeated. "He need not fear shame or punishment, because the thief may have sneaked the money into his pocket. If the money is not surrendered, we'll do a body check on everyone—with all the consequences."

The silence that followed banged off the cement walls.

"I told you," Sommer whispered in my ear. "I'm not surprised."

Neidhart waited. No one spoke. The guards moved forward and arranged the crowd into eight rows. As they frisked each person, he was allowed to leave the room. Kraus sat on a bench, biting his knuckles and goggling at the proceedings through his thick glasses. Waiting for my turn, I thought how little we knew of each other. We all wore the same Merxplas uniform—bank directors and petty clerks, judges and thieves. Everyone was suspect. Even the bank director who had lost his riches might have a chipped conscience—if he ever had an intact one.

Barely half the men were checked when the night bell sounded. Would this emergency allow an exception from the prison rule? Apparently not. To my surprise, Guard Dierx announced it was time to go to bed, thief or no thief.

But there was method in this ruling. In the middle of the night lights went on and an unscheduled bell aroused us from sleep. Guards swarmed in to check our belongings. The unsuspecting thief would now be exposed. Good thinking.

But it didn't work. Nothing was found. At breakfast the air was filled with smoldering suspicion. At my class I could not concentrate on flower making. I thought of various scenarios for what might have happened, none beyond the realm of fiction. Berber, back after his sickness, had lost his whimsical charm. He kept pacing back and forth, hugging his elbow as if shivering. It was a relief when the class was over and we returned to the dayroom. The same haze of despondency hung in the air, occasionally sparked by flickers of rumors, none holding up.

Neidhart motioned me to him. Silently we walked to Holländer's cubbyhole. Benedikt, Stein, and Kraus were there.

Holländer sat woodenly on the only chair in the little room. Pale and bedraggled, he massaged his chin with one hand. We waited. After a while, he said: "We're getting nowhere. Vandenheuvel is a decent man. Bringing in the police would endanger us all. He has given us two weeks. All outgoing mail is being checked. No visitors. We have to find the thief ourselves." Then, turning to Stein: "You have experience with criminals. Will you help?"

Stein blushed with pleasure. "I'll do what I can. If my two colleagues will work with me. You were bluffing about knowing the serial numbers of the banknotes?"

Holländer nodded wretchedly. The Judge turned to Kraus: "When did you miss the money?"

Kraus seemed dissolved in watery misery: teary eyes, moist lips, drops of sweat on his forehead, damp palms. "Yesterday noon."

"Where was it hidden?"

"I kept it in my wallet, in the inside pocket of my jacket." He spoke out of the left corner of his mouth. His whole face was distorted. I wondered if he had suffered a slight stroke.

"And your jacket is locked in your suitcase?" Stein continued.

Kraus banged his forehead with both fists. "I was stupid. Stupid! I wore my jacket Sunday for visitor's day. At night, I hung it on a nail beside my bed. Monday morning I put on my overalls, and forgot about the jacket." He exploded in a fit of fury. "This goddamned rush in the morning, making the bed, then out into that icy darkness, then back to breakfast! I cannot move fast because of my stupid leg, I'm always behind everywhere. I remembered the jacket only in the cobbler class, and wanted to go back to the dorm to lock up my jacket. But that shithead Minkus didn't let me go, and when I got back after class, the money was gone."

"The rules of the camp." Holländer lectured. "No leaving during class."

"Fuck the rules," Kraus said with conviction.

"What else was in the wallet?" Stein asked.

"Not much. Stamps. Calling cards, addresses. A photo of my mother."

"When did you report the loss?"

"As soon as I found out. About 11:20 or so. I told Dierx, and he said he would report it to Vandenheuvel." Another outburst of rage. "Those idiotic Belgian bureaucrats! They took me to the Administration Building and asked a hundred inane questions, and had me fill out forms. I don't read French, they had to translate everything. By the time they searched for the money it was gone."

"The *directeur* had to decide whether to call in the outside police."

"I wonder why he didn't," Benedikt interjected.

"Because that would have shown what an inefficient asshole he is!" Kraus shouted, quivering with fury.

"The money must still be in camp," Benedikt decided.

"And I'll find it!" The Judge's voice was resonant as his blunt fingers gripped my arm. "Get me some sheets from your notebook. I'll find the thief and deliver him to justice!"

A solemn oath to the Goddess of Justice. None of us knew how blind she was.

2.

Stein threw himself into the investigation with the zeal of an unemployed offered work. He spent his free time making lists—suspects, possible scenarios, places where the money could be hidden, ways it could have been smuggled out. He interrogated, made notes of what people said and how they reacted to his questions. He showed a self-assurance he must have had during his years on the bench. He was judge, public prosecutor, chief investigator. He designated Benedikt and me as his assistants and held daily conferences with us.

I have no detailed notes of our conversations but the memories seem to come into sharper focus as I now relive these fifty-year-old events. Stein needed our get-togethers not because we could help, but because it gave him the opportunity to review his notes and detect connections that might have escaped him. What I remember most clearly was how his bearing changed from camp prisoner to judge. He would stalk back and forth, hands clasped in back, head bowed in thought. He would stand silently, hands shoved in his pockets, chin on chest, gnawing his underlip. He would count off possibilities on his fingers, inspecting every finger as if seeing it for the first time. Having thought of a promising lead, he would steeple his fingers in front of his face, tapping the tips together, frowning.

During my apprentice year in a Vienna courthouse I had developed a cynical view of judges— paragraphs walking in robes, I called them. Here I saw a human being trying his best to deal with other human beings. Stein did not take his job lightly. There were tangles of doubt expressed by a crossing and recrossing of legs, a ponderous chewing on his pipe stem, a contemplative pulling of his earlob, a reflective rubbing of his chin— genuine efforts to get hold of a tip of the truth.

"The perpetrator," Stein would say—he loved that word—"the perpetrator could be a student in our class. They knew about the wallet in the jacket hanging in the dorm. Kraus made quite a fuss about leaving class to lock it up.

Benedikt and I guessed Minkus, but Stein would have none of it. He was a firm believer in the presumption of innocence and was collecting evidence, going over and over the sheets in his growing file. He had made a list of the sixteen people in the cobbler class. He had talked to each although, as he pointed out regretfully, he had no power of subpoena. But everyone cooperated. He established that the theft must have occurred between 11 o'clock, when the class ended, and 11:20 when Kraus discovered the money gone. Stein went over the list of cobbler students. Two had gone to the soccer field. Max Hutt confirmed their "testimony." Four others had walked together to the dayroom, and their stories checked out. Two more had gone to the canteen to buy stamps, and Waniek who opened his little shop at 11 sharp was sure they had arrived no later than five after 11, the time required to walk from the cobbler class to the canteen. Stein checked this out by timing his own walk. Stein himself had stayed behind with two more men to clean up. This left five men unaccounted for. Horowitz hit his thumb in class and went to Berman but saw him only half hour later, so could have lifted the money.

"And Minkus?" Benedikt asked again.

Minkus had left the class because he had cramps. He immediately went to the toilets.

"And no one saw him there?" Benedikt insisted.

"No one saw, heard or smelled him there," Stein said with a rare show of humor.

I suggested that anyone in the camp could be the thief. I became interested in this investigation. Here was a crimi in the making.

Stein nodded gravely, plucking more sheets from his file. Beyond the cobbler students, he noted, the prime suspects were the people in our dorm. They would have seen the jacket and may have looked for anything worth lifting.

I couldn't believe the thief would be one of our pioneer transport. These were my friends, the cream of the crop.

But Stein was not excluding anyone, staring at me.

"I'll come clean, Your Honor," Benedikt burlesqued a prime suspect. "At 11, I talked to Holländer about the next visitors day. This," he added with a hint of mischief, "clears our president, too."

"And I stayed behind in my class to finish a daisy," I mimicked Benedikt. "And I have a witness. Berber helped me."

But for Stein this was no joking matter. He made notes, kept comparing them, pulling out additional sheets. The perpetrator, he pointed out, may come from the pool of men who didn't go to classes—the cleaning crew, the kitchen helpers. Even the sick. Lots of work to do.

He wasn't complaining. He had found a purpose.

3.

We met every day for the next week after the evening meal, to listen to Stein's laborious collection of evidence. His file thickened.

"Everyone cooperates," he delighted."The number of suspects is shrinking. Of course, I have to crosscheck every statement. Only Kramrisch refuses to be questioned. He says it's an insult to his integrity."

"Does this make him a suspect?" I asked.

Stein flipped his palm back and forth. "Not necessarily. Kramrisch was a high official in the Justice Department, you know."

"And had to convert to get his position." Benedikt's voice was bitter. "So much for integrity."

But Stein was inclined to discount Kramrisch's refusal. He had learned to spot liars, he claimed.

He patiently went through his lists to find contradictions, loopholes, cross references. He drew conclusions, recapitulated, summarized. It came down to three questions: who, how, and why. The why seemed obvious to me. Money was the key to a new life, even if only in the jungles of some malaria-infested country. I asked myself a disturbing question: would I steal money to buy myself a visa to freedom? More disturbing still: would I steal to save my mother?

I remember these ruminations because they led to the only contribution I was able to make to Stein's investigation. He was lecturing about the importance of finding a motive. The motivation, I replied, was to buy a visa from a corrupt consul of some banana republic. We heard such rumors almost every week. Stein had the utmost contempt for such illegal dealings and discounted them as swindles.

"Remember the day Minkus took over the cobbler class?" I asked Stein. "When he told about buying visas to Paraguay?"

Stein turned his searchlight eyes on me. "That's right. And he mentioned the price of 2,000 francs."

"Didn't he also mention the address where the money had to be sent ?" Benedikt asked.

"Somewhere in Paris," I recalled. "And when Fred Glogau said that no one had that kind of money, Klingenberg told us he knew that Kraus had received money in a letter."

Stein slapped his forehead with his palm. "I'm getting senile," he called out in mock agony.

We tried to remember who was present that day when Kraus's money was mentioned. Klingenberg had spoken in a low voice to make sure Kraus, limping behind, was out of earshot. But all the other cobbler students must have heard it.

"Tell me," Benedikt turned to Stein, "when Kraus asked to leave the class early, did he mention the money in his jacket?"

"Not the amount. He just spoke about money."

To my mind, the mystery novel was on its last page. "It makes no difference whether Kraus mentioned the money or not," I remember saying.

"Minkus knew. At least he knew there was a big chance. He kept Kraus in the class, ran over to the dorm and took the money long before Kraus, with his bad leg, could get there."

But to my disappointment, Stein shook his head. "Any judge would laugh us out of court with such skimpy circumstantial evidence. We have to do better than that. We have to establish a link between Minkus and the money. We have to find the money, fingerprints. It must still be in camp. The only way to sneak it out would be in a letter. The mail is picked up and taken to the Administration Building at 10 a.m., long before Minkus could have lifted it."

I wouldn't give up so easily. "He could have mailed it out the next day," I suggested.

Stein shook his head again. "After the night check, when nothing was found, the outgoing mail has been opened every day. The money still is in camp and we must find it." He turned to me. "If you had money to hide, where would you hide it?" He handed me a sheet from his file. "Here's a list of the places I've checked. Can you think of others?"

I thought this ridiculous.The way the legal mind creates its own mazes! For me, the case was solved. But then I realized that in mystery stories the obvious suspect is never the "perpetrator."

4.

A shower of personal events sidelined my part as Dr.Watson to Stein's Holmes.

A week before Christmas I received the kind of letter every inmate of Merxplas dreamed of. It was from the American Consulate in Antwerp and said in three lines that my affidavit of support had arrived from Mrs. Sophie Beck, South Orange, New Jersey, and that I should come to the Consulate December 20, at 10 a.m.

A drizzly mist enwrapped the camp, but for me it was a day of blinding sunshine. Sophie Beck was the widow of my long-lost relative in America my father had discovered and contacted. My sand castles had found firm ground! Guiltily I looked around at the seething wretchedness around me and repressed my joy behind clenched teeth. I had never been so happy in my life. I *had* to share my news with someone. Clutching the letter I went to Benedikt who was playing chess with Neidhart.

When I told them, I saw the warmth in Benedikt's eyes and felt his shared delight in the silent clasp of his hands. Neidhart's reaction was immediate and practical. "You must get a pass from Vandenheuvel right away. Tell Dierx. Then we'll announce it."

My first reaction was violently negative. There was an age-long superstition in our family (and especially in my mother) that you don't announce happy events because this will cast a spell on them and make them not come true. But Neidhart saw it differently. My letter would be a ray of hope for all those who were at various stages of waiting for an American visa. Benedikt understood my hesitation but also urged me to include the happy news in my next bulletin. It would lift the spirit of the "community."

Everything went swimmingly. I got my one-day pass, and the original Merxplas dogcatcher #1 took me to Tournhout where I went by bus to Antwerp. When I arrived at the American Consulate at about 9:30, I joined a line of applicants waiting for the door to open. They all were in their Sunday best, men in freshly pressed suits under heavy overcoats, some women in fur coats, the most precious possession they had been able to take with them. I remembered the long lines of cowering people in front of the various consulates in Vienna, hoping to get in before a passing brownshirt had his fun kicking them or forcing them back to the end of the line. In Vienna, the consulates were impregnable castles with moats all around. Here, in Antwerp, the American Consulate was a draw bridge leading to freedom.

Everyone was chatting excitedly. We came from different pasts but were united in our hopes for a future. My story was not unique. Everyone talked about rediscovered cousins, namesakes found in telephone books, helpful strangers. For those waiting, America was still undiscovered. We had only the vaguest ideas about it. I asked a squat, chubby-faced man how far South Orange was from Hollywood—I fantasized using the affidavit from "aunt" Sophie to get to the United States, and my connection with Dave Epstein to start my writing career in Hollywood.

The doors of the Consulate opened at 10 sharp and we bustled into a hallway where everybody got a number. We lined up on a long bench along the wall, according to our number. We sat there, chirpily like birds on a telegraph wire. Next to me, a short and peppy man announced cheerfully that he had a job waiting for him in a dentist's office in Chicago.

"For heaven's sakes," said the man on his other side, "don't tell this to the Consul, or you'll never get in."

I learned that American law stipulated that immigrants must not have a job before entry. Several people sitting on the bench, like know-it-all Sommer, knew all the facts. America still had its depression. It also was a free country. Once there, you could take any job you could get. But you must not have a job before the visa was granted. It made no sense to me—but what immigration laws did? In England, women could get a visa only if they *did* have a domestic job contract before entry. In America, if you were lucky enough to have a job contract, you had to enter the land of unlimited possibilities with a lie.

All this didn't worry me. I had no job, only aunt Sophie and my namesake in Hollywood.

From time to time the door to the inner sanctum opened and a uniformed guard let the person with the next number enter. The others slid up the bench, closer to the door. The line moved amazingly quickly. Getting the visa seemed to be a mere formality. Or were they gathering inside to fill out forms, getting fingerprinted, sworn in? Anyway, no one came out whom we could ask about the mysteries behind the closed door.

Finally, my number was called and the guard motioned me in. A secretary in a bright-flowered dress studied a folder on her desk through huge horn-rimmed glasses. She had gray, carefully coiffeured hair and carmine, almond-shaped finger nails.

"Sophie Beck," she read, tracing the lines in the document with a sharply pointed pencil. "South Orange, New Jersey. How exactly is she related to you?"

This could be a trap. I didn't know, my father didn't know. Sophie probably didn't know, either.

"She is the sister of my grandfather," I said boldly.

She didn't seem disturbed and scribbled something on the document in front of her. "Have you been in written contact with her?"

"Yes," I lied.

"How long?"

"Ever since I can remember." I felt light-hearted, ready to tell her stories. She was in no position to know. "She's sent me birthday presents every year."

Maybe this was too rash. For a split second I felt a leap of panic, but the well-groomed grandma kept leafing through my file, underlining words, scribbling marginal notes.

"One moment." She took my file and left the room through a heavily ornamented oak door. She had never once looked at me. Suddenly the fire ball in my stomach flared up, as it did more and more frequently. All seemed to go well but for a moment I was afraid I would vomit. I clenched my fists and dug the nails in my palm.

The secretary returned with my file and settled comfortably in her chair. She looked at me. For the first time I could see her pale-blue, expressionless eyes.

"Your affidavit is all right," she announced, and I wondered how a person could be so unsmilingly noncommittal when she brought such wonderful news. 'Your quota number is a few months off. This gives you time to fulfill the requirements."

My stomach clenched again.

"What requirements?"

"The Consul requires a $3,000 blocked account in an American bank."

"But I have a guarantor," I protested.

"Guarantees are easily given," she said woodenly, "and easily broken."

I argued, as a lawyer, a published writer, a human being. I might as well have argued with a recording machine. With a display of long-suffering patience, she responded to arguments she must have heard hundreds of times. True, the law demanded only a sponsor, but it also gave each consul the right to make additional conditions. A blocked account meant the money could be drawn only in small monthly amounts over three years. The United States was suffering from a depression, thousands were unemployed. Even native writers could not sell their stories. The economy was strained. The government had to protect its citizens.

I feverishly thought of arguments that would convince her. She merely drummed her carmine-tipped fingers on the desk, looking right through me as if I were air. I wanted to grab her well-rounded shoulders and shake her. I tried hard to keep myself under control, and asked to talk to the Consul myself. The Consul was not available.

"Please go now," she said, with a shrug of regret. "Many others are waiting."

"They'll be waiting all their lives," I snapped at her.

She shut my file and put it aside. "We'll talk again when you bring evidence of your blocked account."

5.

I was let out a side door. A huddle of the rejects was lingering in a hallway, commiserating. They looked harrowed, gaunt, defeated—the way I felt myself. A frail woman with red-rimmed eyes mumbled over and over again, "what will happen to us?" A pouchy man, collapsed into a slouch of self-pity, tried to reassure himself by repeating, "There *must* be a way." An old man, with tight, pale lips, said in a thin, nasal, whiny voice, "Someone told me, but I didn't believe it. The new consul in Antwerp is an anti-Semite. He makes it impossible to get a visa. He asked a $5,000 blocked account for me and my wife. Blocked for three years! I can't ask my sponsor. She's not a rich woman."

Everybody in the room mentioned his own, fatal figure: $3,000, $5,000, $8,000— astronomical figures for us. How could we ask strangers, even relatives, to deposit this kind of money? (In 1938 you could buy a house in America for $5,000.)

I was suffocating in this thick fog of despair and left. The air outside was brisk and cold. I tried to breath in deeply but my throat constricted. I felt dizzy, afraid I would faint. I grabbed the iron railing next to the steps to the street.

Then I heard a faint voice, calling my name. A few steps away stood a female figure wrapped in a cloth coat. She smiled at me and crooked a forefinger, beckoning me closer.

It was Karla Berman.

6.

We rushed into each other's arms like old lovers. I hung onto her as to a life belt. I breathed in her fragrance—no perfume, just young, clean femininity. With every breath health and hope flooded in. The weight was lifted. I thirstily sought her mouth, and for a divine moment the American Consul faded into obscurity. The future paled into unimportance. This was one of the few moments in my life when I was all present. And it was heavenly.

For years I rationalized that this abrupt leap from hell to heaven explained my inexcusable obtuseness that morning. It was 11:30. My bus to Tournhout left at 3. This gave us three-and-a-half hours to make love. My friendship with Berman was forgotten by my deep need to fill my frustration with this vibrant, inviting body.

We had lunch in a little restaurant. She had learned at the Committee of my being at the American Consulate in Antwerp today, and she came to see me. That's all I heard. That's all I wanted to hear. Only much later did I realize what it was she was trying to tell me, what was really important to her. She spoke of her husband's urging her to see Louis Pluvier, to get medical supplies, a hospital room for the camp. She spoke of her hate of the poverty of emigration, the Committee hand-outs, the shared attic with Susi. I heard her throaty voice but not the desperate message. She spoke of Louis Pluvier, the rich playboy, whose mother did volunteer work at the Committee.

"Teddy wants me to go to Pluvier and ask for help." Karla repeated the sentence in various forms. "He thinks Pluvier can get him all he needs."

"All he needs," she repeated sadly and wiped tears from her lashes. I didn't know why she cried and why she told me all these things. I heard her words through my starved glands, and saw only those sparkling eyes, those pouty lips, the slender throat, the coral flesh above her cleavage.

"Tell me, is that heatable room really so important to Ted? " she implored me.

"Oh yes, yes," I said, pressing her hand and hungrily kissing her palm.

"Oh, Joe," she breathed. "Do you want to make love to me?"

I was startled by her question. I thought this was understood. I quickly paid for the food, and she followed me demurely to a small hotel in the neighborhood.

7.

My news from the American Consulate had a devastating effect in Merxplas. Contrary to what Neidhart had expected, my report smashed the hopes for all those who held American quota numbers and waited for affidavits.

We held a meeting, attended by bitter, savage, explosive men. Wolf, Weinkraut, and their gang did their police work and kept order. Proposals were made and discarded. A cable to President Roosevelt was drafted, but even the sparsest wording cost more than we could hope to raise. Eventually a letter was sent to the Jewish Relief Committee in New York but never achieved results.

It was a sad Christmas. The camp administration tried to put up a small Christmas tree but this was violently rejected by the handful of the orthodox. Most of us were emancipated Jews, and Christmas had no religious connotations. When I was a child, we did have a tree, with real candles, chains of silver-colored walnuts, and home-made cookies hanging from its branches. This was mostly the influence of my Catholic nursemaid who stayed with us until her death when I was fifteen. My parents did not object to the tree and gave me small presents, but it never approached the significance of birthdays. Most inmates in Merxplas felt neutral about Christmas. Siegfried Neumann and Franz Jäger presented a skit by Karl Farkas and Fritz Grünbaum, two Jewish Viennese authors. After all, Jäger pointed out in his introduction, Jesus was a Jew.

8.

Shortly after Christmas, Stein took Benedikt and me aside, his dark eyes dancing. "I know how the money was smuggled out !" He paused dramatically. "It was sent in a letter."

He had checked with the guards who took our mail to the Administration Building. It was picked up at 10 every morning from the makeshift box in Waniek's canteen, but what we didn't know was that it often stayed for hours in the guards' room. Stein located the guard in charge of the mail on that particular Monday, and learned that it had remained in the guards' room until about 2 p.m., enough time for the stolen money to be put in an envelope and added to the box. Stein had not been able to ascertain for sure if the guards' room was unattended during that time, but this was often the case.

I was not overly impressed. "Suppose this is what happened," I said. "It only means we'll never find the money, nor fingerprints. How will we find the thief?"

Stein sat, hunched forward, intent, a wound-up spring. "I've narrowed the number of suspects down to nine" he said with a sniff of pride. "Not bad in a crowd of 600. In a sardine box like this, few people can do anything unobserved. People from the training groups usually walk back to the main buildings together. Some, like the farmers, couldn't even make it back before 11:20. The serving crews stick together. I checked and cross-checked to see if individuals left the groups during the critical time. Only nine have no confirmed alibi. A pretty negative evidence, I admit. But it's something to work on."

Stein spread out what he called his 'goniff list', mostly people I knew well.

The cobblers were high on the list. He pointed his sharp pencil to one name at a time. Minkus was the prime suspect. The whereabouts between 11 and 11:30 was also unconfirmed for Horowitz who left the class to see Bermann about his thumb. Glogau had run off to complain to Holländer about the way Minkus had treated Stein that morning but had not reached Holländer until later. Kramrisch refused to be interviewed because he considered it insulting. A newcomer, Soffer, had left the electrician class to look for a cardboard box behind the kitchen but was not seen there by anyone. Kaiser of the Spanish class, and Tischler, a barber student, had given vague and contradictory testimonies. And finally, there was the guard who took the mail to the Aministration Building.

The guard?

"Nobody's excluded," Stein stated firmly.

"Any particular suspect?" Benedikt wanted to know.

"Not directly." Stein peered over the rim of his glasses and lowered his voice. "Minkus has become mean to me."

"Guilty conscience?" Benedikt guessed.

"Could be." Stein cleared his throat ostentatiously and explained that psychology could provide leads as strong as fingerprints. Minkus had been surprisingly friendly to Stein at first. He wanted to be a pal. Stein didn't welcome his chumminess and, since the theft, Minkus had become increasingly nasty. Stein admitted that he was not the most gifted of cobbler students, and by far the oldest. Minkus lost no opportunity to mock Stein, sneeringly calling him "Your Honor." It upset Glogau more than it upset Stein. Glogau was really the reason for Stein's staying in the class. The man and the boy had become extremely close, spent all their time together. Glogau had even taken to call Stein "Uncle Richard." In the cobbler class they sat together and the boy helped the older man whenever he could. Cobblers, when repairing soles, stretch the shoe over a metal last to hammer the nails in. In Merxplas, they didn't have boot-lasts and held the shoe on their knees while hammering. Minkus went from student to student to show how this was done. Minkus banged on Stein's knee harder than on anyone else's, making remarks like, "It was more comfy to sit on a judge's bench, wasn't it, Your Honor?" On the day of the theft, when Stein hammered the shoe on his knee, his whole thigh began to twitch, he couldn't control it. Minkus broke into a hoarse laugh, pointing gleefully at the jerking leg. "Give up, Stein," he roared. "Maybe you got what it takes to be a judge. It's not good enough for cobbler apprentice." He whacked Stein on the back and knocked him off the stool. That's why Fred ran to complain to Holländer.

9.

I lost interest in Stein's investigation. I lost interest in everything — in flower making, even in short-story writing. I felt a volcano of irritability in my stomach, and I felt weak and sick. I went through the daily camp routines like in a trance. At the far end of my consciousness I was aware of the shoutings, the kiddings, the flare-ups, the efficient rulings of the Wolf gang. I became an outsider in Benedikt's emergent community of sufferers. My old friends tried to include me, but I withdrew. Berman's attempts to help only intensified my despair by the memory of what I had done to him.

I remember very little about these days, and have no notes. It needed a few kicks of fate to bring me back.

The first was a letter Berman received. His application for Australia had been rejected. He and Karla had had a chance, he said, his face creased with misery. Somehow, this rejection made my guilt heavier. These were the first days of 1939. I had a foreboding that it would be a terrible year, perhaps my last.

The mail was being distributed. I received a letter from Max in London who tried to comfort me by saying he would find a way to get me to England to wait for my quota number there. The American Embassy in London made no additional demands. To get to England, I knew, was as hopeless as all else.

Suddenly I became aware of eddies of excitement around Paul Schramek who handed out the letters.

Bernard Klein came by. "Minkus got a visa! To South America!"

I jolted to attention. "To Paraguay?"

Klein raised his shoulders in a gesture of resignation. "Paraguay, Uruguay, Bolivia—who cares? Away from this stinkhole!"

But I cared a lot. I shouldered my way through the clutch of people surrounding Minkus. Wolf, Weinkraut, Jonatai, the whole gang was there, cheering. Minkus waved some papers in triumph. He spotted Stein, and made his way to him.

"Hey, Your Honor," he shouted, with a slap of ostentatious camaraderie. "Three cheers for His Honor!" He turned to his friends. "To whom do I owe this visa? None other than His Honor! You know where I met the guy who got it for me? In the clink where His Honor sent me! A swell pal, Nick. He had a bit of a past, so he went to Chile. That was easy, two years ago. Now he sent me a visa. See, Your Honor, if you had gone to the clink instead of sending *me* there, you could go to Chile, instead of rotting here!"

Stein's ashen face showed no bitterness, no self-pity. He surprised me by offering his hand to Minkus, in a silent wish of luck. My own stomach juices began to bubble again and I raced outside to get fresh air. My brain felt ravaged as a fruit is by a worm. How could Stein still believe in justice? The world was plunged in a morass of injustice. Nazi Germany was leading the spooky reign, and other countries followed. The nationalists triumphed in Spain, the Japanese in China, the Italians in Abyssinia. Austria no longer existed, Czechoslovakia was being abandoned. In Palestine, Jews were barred from their last hope for asylum. Berman was condemned to perish, Minkus was allowed a fresh start. Justice, 1939.

10.

Two days later, at lunch time before mail distribution, Fred Glogau stormed into the dining hall, grabbed Stein's hand, and pulled him off his bench.

"Uncle Richard," he shouted. "An express letter! You got an express letter!"

Stein disentangled his legs from the others under the table to climb clumsily over the bench. "How do you know?"

The boy's laughter exploded, unheralded like a jumping fish. "I checked with Schramek. A letter from Zürich!"

"I don't know anybody in Zürich," Stein mumbled, while the boy pulled him away.

The soup was being dished out. The incident didn't get much attention, except at our table. I took a few spoonfuls, then my curiosity got the better of me. Something extraordinary was going on.

Stein sat on a bench in the deserted dayroom, reading a letter. Fred was watching him like an excited puppy. Schramek was readying his carton of regular mail.

Stein's heavy face sagged, the letter dangled from his lifeles hand. If Fred had not supported him he would have fallen off the bench.

"Is it from Kurt?" Fred asked eagerly. "Is it from Kurt?"

The judge did not reply. He handed the letter to me. Fred jumped behind me and looked at the letter over my shoulders.

"Dearest father," the letter read, "I am free, free, free! I knew you could do it. Mother got the notification from the Paraguayan consulate only last week, and she sent in my passport. Aunt Lottie helped me get bookings from Marseille. I won't thank you with words but by working hard so you can join me soon. Love and thousand kisses, and thanks, thanks, thanks! Your Kurti."

Stein sat still, only his leg began to jerk. He stared emptily at Fred who was all over him, hugging and kissing.

"It worked!" the boy shouted. "Kurt is free, will become rich, you'll join him. Everything will be all right. It was simple, wasn't it?"

I had never before seen a man disintegrate before my eyes. Everything in him slumped, his shoulders, head, fingers.

"Aren't you happy?" Fred chattered. "Here you get the best news in the world, and you aren't happy. What's wrong?"

"Go finish your lunch, my boy," Stein said, his voice breaking. "We'll talk later."

Fred bent down, kissed the judge's cheek, and with a confused and questioning glance at me, left. Stein sat, staring at his trembling leg. I felt I was looking into a secret place where I had no business. Yet I didn't want to leave the judge alone.

"I have failed," he said, wanly.

"You couldn't possibly know," I tried, but he waved me aside.

"No, no. I don't mean that." A long pause. Then: "I failed in that, too. My love made me blind to the obvious. But that's not what matters. I failed as a father, a person, a *Mensch*." He used that untranslatable German-Jewish word that expresses the humanity of a human being. "I failed my only child and chased after a stolen wallet and the phantom of justice. I'm the dinosaur of our age. Fred is a child of our times and he acted. He acted in a way I damn and detest, but he saved Kurt."

I didn't know what to say. But Stein was not even aware of my presence. His mind had drifted far away, into another world. "I always could tell right from wrong," he said, his voice barely audible. "I can't any more. I don't know the new moral laws." Another long pause. "I believed in eternal moral laws." He laced his fingers in desperation. "I still believe in them. But if there is divine justice why does God allow its earthly sister to be strangled?"

Here was a man whose world had shattered. He was a rational man and found it unbearable to face the irrational. He hated untidiness and now his life was a jumble. I wanted to help but was utterly helpless. "We have to have faith," I said, not believing it myself.

Stein sadly shook his massive head. "Faith in a world where a criminal laughs at his judge and is rewarded? Where an honest man is ashamed of his honesty, and a cheater boasts about his cheating? Where a boy steals and cannot comprehend the man who disapproves? And the man who disapproves is a fool because theft brings life, and honesty death."

"What are you going to do?" I asked.

"I don't know." He heaved himself awkwardly to his feet. "I have never in my life sentenced anyone to death."

11.

I wanted to stay with Stein during the afternoon, skipping my class, but he firmly said no. He himself remained in the dayroom, going through the formality of getting permission to be excused from cobbler class.

"I have to do some thinking," he told me, and looking intently into my eyes, added: "No word to anyone, please."

I spent a fretful afternoon, making useless flowers from wire and wool, and was relieved to find Stein in the dayroom, gracefully receiving congratulations for the rescue of his son.

Benedikt took me aside. "Paraguay? Isn't that strange?"

I agreed it was strange, but said nothing.

The next morning the wake-up bell shrilled, and Neidhart went through his daily chore to shake awake the tardy. When he came to Stein's bed he quickly ran over to Berman. I went with him and immediately saw what had happened.

I had never seen a dead body. My parents protected me from all sadness, even spared me attending my grandfather's funeral. But Judge Stein's face was serene and peaceful. He was dead, all doubts dissolved, all questions answered.

Stein's suitcase gaped open under his cot. A trunkful of litter that were the judge's sole possessions.

Holländer was called, Vandenheuvel, the camp physician. They found Kurt's letter, the empty bottle of sleeping pills. No final note.

"Who would have thought . . . " people said. " . . terrible . . . unbelievable . . . The only way to save his son . . . but he, a former judge . . no one can see into someone else . . . he has judged himself. "

Kraus screamed and stormed when he realized his money was gone for good, and Fred Glogau sobbed uncontrollably. When he saw me, he clutched me frantically, as if drowning.

"Why?" he moaned. "Why did he do it? When everything worked out so well? Can you understand this?"

IX. The Price of a Sickroom

I.

I find an entry in my old notes: "Stein's suicide tore a gap in my life." It sounds dramatic. I knew the man only three months. Yet, the sentence contained more truth than I suspected at the time. Through this gap I glimpsed a reality I had never before seen.

I cried that night on my lonely cot. I hadn't cried when I left my parents, not in the prison cell, not at my deportation to Merxplas. So far, everything had been softened by my belief in a fairy godmother who would make all come out right. But death was dreadfully and hopelessly final. I cried knowing I wasn't crying about Judge Stein. I cried for myself. About all the things that had died in my life. My family. My career. My friends. My Viennese leading lady. My country. My language. My future. Perhaps we always cry only for ourselves, our ultimate loneliness, our unsolvable conflicts, the inexplicability of life. The outline of a story formed itself in my mind, a story that wouldn't sell to British papers but I knew I had to write. About an Austrian judge who fled to America. His brother, who also emigrated to America, told him in great excitement that he had found the love of his life in New York. She was a great beauty who had arrived from Vienna before the Nazi take-over. She was non-Jewish, the widow of a wealthy Austrian aristocrat. Her reasons for fleeing were political. When the judge met the lady, he remembered her well. He also knew the "political" reasons for her escape: she had been accused of poisoning her husband and stood trial in a Vienna court. She very likely was guilty but the jury acquitted her. It had been quite a scandal in Austria. The brother didn't know, but the judge did. Now, in America, she implored him to keep her secret, swore she was innocent and loved his brother deeply. The judge didn't know what to do, and neither did I. I worked on this story for years, picked it up again and again, trying alternate solutions. It wouldn't let me come to rest. It's still in my file of unfinished stories.

2.

A few days after Stein's death a chauffeur-driven Mercedes stopped at the hedge near Pavilion A and a dapper young man stepped from it. Looking out over the big red brick building, he stood wrapped in a flapping camel-hair coat, legs apart, arms akimbo, a bemused smile curling his lips under a thin mustache.

"Louis Pluvier," Klingenberg gasped. "Rich, influential. Let's make an excuse to meet him. Interview him. I'll go with you."

I approached the rose-cheeked youth, notebook in hand, pencil drawn. He was a pretty boy, wearing a tawny fedora, his lank blond hair falling carelessly over his forehead. He examined me from deep-set eyes under long lashes.

"Newsletter?" he snickered. "What's it called? *Le Monde de Merxplas* ?

Stick with me, boys. I'll give you a story. Where do I find this Berman character?"

I disliked him immediately. But Klingenberg bowed and scraped. "The doctor is in his office."

"Do I need an appointment?"

I would have liked to kick him but Klingenberg managed a dutiful chuckle.

Berman, in his medical cubbyhole, was tapping a man's bare back with his finger. He didn't look up when we entered.

"Monsieur Louis Pluvier wants to see you," Klingenberg announced ceremoniously like a butler in a play. Berman grunted, putting his ear on the man's back. Suddenly he straightened up and his face brightened.

"Pluvier?" He briefly turned back to his patient. "You can get dressed now. Two aspirins, as yesterday. Stay near the oven in the dayroom. Here's your release slip from class for two weeks." He extended a meaty hand to Pluvier. "Welcome to Merxplas Medical Center." He made a sweeping gesture about the wobbly shelf with bottles and pill boxes next to the fold-up cot. "The man who just left has pneumonia. We need a heated sickroom desperately. And medical supplies. I don't even have a stethoscope."

Pluvier focused his whimsical look on the stout, solid figure in the white coat: "So you are Dr. Theodor Berman, husband of Karla." He scanned the small room. "She didn't exaggerate. It's a dump. You have a very persuasive spokeswoman, Berman." Unexpectedly, he giggled.

"Let me show you the camp," Berman said. "You can see under what conditions we operate."

Pluvier squiggled uncomfortably but Berman determinedly opened the door for him. Whistling Pluvier left the room, whistling he walked through the dayroom, the dorms, the washroom — distant, unconcerned, like a visitor in a museum that didn't interest him. He never asked a question, never took notes or asked me, as Helen Pleienberg had done, to take notes for him. He paid no attention to me, or Klingenberg, or even Berman who patiently explained his needs. He kept looking at his wristwatch and after a few minutes slipped away to his car. Berman was crestfallen. He handed Pluvier a list of his most urgent needs, and Pluvier, with his dainty fingers, handed it to his chauffeur. He climbed into the backseat, rolled down the window, stuck his head out, and told Berman in his velvety vibrato voice: "Don't worry. I'll take care of everything."

I could tell that Berman did not believe a word. In a last effort to pin down something he asked: "Do you have any idea how long it will take?"

Pluvier seemed amused by the question. "No time at all," he said lightly. "There's no reason for delay." Again he giggled as if he knew of a joke from which we were excluded.

I thought I knew what the joke was, and felt unhappy and guilty.

3.

Three days later, I got a scoop for my newsletter. Director Vandenheuvel told Berman the hospital room was approved, and a representative of a medical-supply house was here to take orders. The cobwebs of bureaucracy had been swept away by one wave of Pluvier's dainty hand.

"A miracle!" Klingenberg enthused, his jowls and wattles jiggling. "God moves in mysterious ways!"

Berman's face was luminous with joy. He looked ten years younger. "He sure does," he beamed. "It would save Him a lot of trouble, though, if he did not send us diseases in the first place."

He conferred with the man from the medical supply house and reported later that all his requests were granted.

The fairy godmother was alive and well, and took on the strangest shapes. Yet the fast delivery only increased my misgivings.

The eight-bed hospital room was housed in the brick church behind Pavilion A, comfortably heated and equipped with space for the pharmaceutical staples Berman had ordered. Our pharmacist, Robert Klimt, stalked about on stork legs and inspected the supplies with the worried look that was his trademark. There was also a broom-closet-sized office for Berman and Kruger to see outpatients.

"What we need," Berman said, "are nurses. God forgot about those."

Kurt Berber took me by surprise by saying impishly, "No, he didn't." Then, turning to me: "What d'you think, Joe, about us becoming nurses? That class of mine goes down the pit anyway, we have four students left. Let's make one last grandiose funeral wreath and do something for the living."

Thus, Berber and I became nurses at Merxplas General Hospital. It was a relatively quiet place and could have solved my problem of constantly having to look for a nook to write my stories. But, strangely, whatever juices I had that produced whimsical short shorts had dried out. I listened to patients pour out their hearts, fears, hopes, doubts — the cruel, senseless, improbable stories that life writes. The bodies lying in these beds could be treated by pills and tonics, but their souls needed a different kind of remedy. Here, Berber was a master medicine man.

"January 12 will be declared a holiday in the Republic Merxplas," he chattered, putting a mustard plaster on one of the patients. "St. Louis Day, in honor of Pluvier of Assissi. You'll see, next year we'll all have a day off."

"Hey, listen," came a protest from one of the beds. "You don't think we'll still be here a year from now?"

Remarks like these released a deluge of therapeutic mock insults from Berber. "What do *you* think, you constipated baboon? You want out? Ha! You'll still celebrate the twenty-fifth anniversary in Merxplas. Berman will be retired but Willy Kruger will give you your two aspirins. Holländer will have a crown on his hairless and brainless head. I have a feeling, Merxplas will become a monarchy. The imperial orb will be a coffee cup, and the sceptre a dried herring. Benedikt will have a long beard and still believe he can create a model democracy here. Klingenberg will be chief rabbi and Wolf in charge of the torture chamber. Waniek will wobble his head and say, "Remember the good old times when Hitler ruled Germany? We had it good, *then*. And we'll assemble in the library and vote whether to write a request to the Committee to get us overseas visas."

Berber moved about the beds with the grace of a dancer which even the bulky Merxplas uniform couldn't hide. He could cheer up the gloomiest patients, and make them take their medication. He cured by insults voiced with disarming charm. When someone fretted over what he had lost, Berber would put on an act of rabid anger and shout: "Now what d'you know? The Herr Direktor has to shine his own shoes! Give me an onion, so I can cry! They probably pulled you out from your mother's womb with sugar-tongs, and Caruso sang at your crib. You had a house, I know, a bird house with a canary in it, and you traveled in a car, a baby buggy! But now you are a big fat zero, and five years from now you'll sit under a tree in the jungle of Peru, nibble on a root, and remember the happy times when you got a dried old herring and were nursed to health by Berber." But if someone was seriously ill, he stayed with him and saw to it that the others were quiet. And when one of our patients had a nightmare and fearfully called for his mother, tears rolled down Berber's cheeks.

4.

Sunday, January 29, was visitors day again. The ban was lifted. Spots of color among the Merxplas drab uniforms, florid dresses, cascading hair, chirpy voices, hugs and kisses. Yet, for me it wasn't the same. I find an entry in my old notes: "Will I ever find a comrade in love?"

A comrade in love. At the first visit I had seen a lot of happy endings—well, at least happy moments. Now I saw couples, haggardly, frazzled, talking about visas, hopeless, with expressionless eyes, voices rising with concern. Benedikt and Natascha, my role models, talked earnestly, heads together, he leaning forward, chin on one hand, she holding the other, her eyes wide open, blue, and participating. Susi Kruger seemed distant, confused, nibbling at her little-girl's mouth, hardly listening to her husband. Berta Holländer followed her man who busily stalked about importantly, giving audiences. She eventually sat down with a thump, all by herself, folding her arms belligerently. Karla Berman did not come.

I felt alone. I missed Judge Stein and the gap was painful. But there was more. I went to the sickroom. Berman examined a patient, four more were waiting. When I had a chance, I asked him, "Where is Karla?"

He put his newly acquired stethoscope into the pocket of his white coat. "She wasn't feeling well. She sent word through Susi."

The fire in my stomach flared up again. "I don't feel so good myself," I moaned.

"Nervous stomach," he decided. "They promised me a gastroscope. As soon as I get it, I'll examine you."

I didn't know what a gastroscope was, but Berman was busy with his next patient. Berber was on duty in the sickroom and I went back to the day room. It was drizzling outside, damp and cold, graveyard weather that fitted my mood. I saw Susi sitting alone and shouldered my way through the cankerous crowd.

"What's wrong with Karla?" I asked.

To my consternation she gushed into tears.

"The baby?" I guessed.

She nodded, wiping her eyes with the heels of both hands.

I tried to say the 'sensible' things. About being young. Getting settled first. Having a family later.

She shook her head so vigorously her blond tresses flew about her thin shoulders. "We'll *never* be settled. Everything's coming to an end."

I tried to argue, not convinced myself. She hardly listened. She sat stiffly like a mannequin. "I lied to Ted," she said. "Karla left."

"What do you mean?" I knew exactly what she meant. "Did she say anything?"

"She didn't have to. A few days ago, she came home drunk. Well, not really drunk. Tipsy. With an expensive dress, and a turquoise necklace."

"Did she say who gave it to her?"

"No," Susi shrugged. "Does it matter? The world is going to pot."

Kruger came bouncing back. "Ted gave me the afternoon off. There's a mob of patients waiting but he says he can handle them. He's got his hospital now."

He didn't know at what price.

5.

Shortly afterwards Holländer, with the air of Siegfried, the dragon-slayer, announced that the Belgian government granted us a two-day furlough every four weeks. Forty men at one time. The Merxplas dogcatcher would take the first batch to Brussels, and two days later bring them back to pick up the next group.

This was a red-letter day, a festival, a communal funfair. But an unexpected problem developed. It was easy to agree on the sequence of the furloughers. We had numbers according to time of arrival, and the first forty would go first. But it turned out that the Belgian government, which had freely transported us to the camp, now charged for the use of the dogcatcher. The Committee had rented the van for the two women visits but didn't have the money for a continuous shuttle.

An emergency meeting of the trustees brought flashes of anger. The 15 francs demanded from each furlougher was almost one-third of the weekly allowance the Committee paid to those living in Brussels, but we in Merxplas received nothing. We suspected, probably rightly, that the government, as well as the Committee, wanted to keep down the numbers of refugees in Brussels. I remembered Dr. Siebenschein's furtive glances and jittery warnings: "No gatherings! No speaking German!" A charge of 15 francs would cut down the potential attention-getters.

"We'll have a riot on our hands," warned Neidhart, "if we limit the visits to those who have the money. Either all go, or none."

"Then we'll also have a riot on our hands," Benedikt predicted. "What do you want us to do? Go on strike?

"This would offend the Committee," Klingenberg cautioned. "We have been asking for this furlough for a long time. It wasn't easy for the Committee to get permission. After all, it's better for some to go than none."

"No, it isn't," Neidhart countered. "A fine community we are. This would be the end of it. You can't exclude people just because they have no money."

"That's the way it is everywhere in the world," Klingenberg stated. "Those who can afford it, go on vacation. The others don't."

"Everywhere in the world, but not here." There was a spice of bitterness in Neidhart's voice. "We wanted to prove something, didn't we? Well, we'd prove that we are as corrupt as the rest of the world."

We argued, eventually voted. Fifteen for, forteen against, one abstention. "So that's decided." Klingenberg stroked his beard in approval. "The first forty who wish to pay can go."

But there was surprising opposition, even from trustees who had the money. Benedikt had voted no, but I could see he was unhappy. If I had a Natascha waiting in Brussels, I would have been unhappy, too.

"This will bust this camp wide open," Neidhart predicted. "We are playing democracy on a barrel of dynamite."

After a babble of confused arguments, in a moment of silence, everybody looked at Benedikt. I had never seen him so uncomfortable. He swallowed hard, his Adam's apple bobbing up and down.

"How much money do we have in the kitty?" he asked George Kellner, formerly of the Rothschild bank in Frankfurt, now our camp treasurer.

Kellner took a notebook from his pocket and adjusted his horn-rimmed glasses. "One hundred fifty francs and fifty cents," he reported gravely.

"That takes care of ten fares," Benedikt said. "I hope this will do for those in the first transport who don't have the funds." When Kellner harrumphed in preparation of a protest, Benedikt explained: "I'll take this up with Madame Pleienberg. She'll replenish your treasury."

He sounded strangely serious. Not a trace of irony in his voice.

"What about future trips?" Neidhart insisted.

"She'll find a way," Benedikt promised, his voice flat and tired.

After everybody filed out of the library room, I held him back.."Why didn't you suggest this in the first place? Why all this hassle?"

He said nothing for a long time, staring vacantly beyond me. Then, with an abrupt resolve, he said, barely audible, "Come outside."

A haloed sun shimmered through the haze. A soccer game was in progress but the pathway along the hedge was empty. He took out a cigarette and spent a long time lighting it, inhaling gratefully, blowing out a plume, removing a bit of tobacco from his lip. Then he started suddenly, a spluttering monologue.

"We talked in the warehouse, Helen and I. As usual, I told her what we needed. As usual, she promised. I don't know how, but the word 'happiness' came up. All of a sudden the dam broke. She talked, I think she didn't even know I was there. About her childhood. A country estate in East Prussia, away from the cities. There she grew up, a tomboy, rumpled hair, swimming in creeks, climbing trees. When she was twelve, Pleienberg came to visit her parents. He was a candidate for some provincial election and Helen's father supported him. He got elected. He impressed her like the boy who could climb the highest tree. Mother asked her if she liked him. She said yes. Could she imagine, when she had grown up, to live with him like mother and father? Yes, again. There was an aura of power and strength about him. He was fourteen years older, twenty-six. They shipped her off to a boarding school where she was trained for society life. At seventeen she was polished. Her wedding was a carnival. She was a princess. The boys with whom she had played looked at her from a distance. They moved to Berlin. Invitations, suppers, balls, theaters. She learned to smile, say the right words, fake, lie. Whatever she did, was to further Pleienberg's career. He was her first and only man. She saw with his eyes, his opinions were hers. She thought this was love."

Benedikt stubbed out his cigarette on his heel. I wondered why he was telling me all this. He stared, without seeing, at the soccer field, the pavilions, the brick church in the distance. Eventually he returned to me. His words came more slowly now.

"Then she said something strange. 'Our emigration opened my eyes,' she said, 'although nothing had changed.' At that time, emigrees still could take everything along, money, possessions, ambitions, the whole sham. Pleienberg's old life emigrated with him. He became a Belgian citizen, wanted to run for office. His help for Merxplas was a rung in his career.

"Helen actually said she wished they'd crossed the border poor. Poor people have something to live for, she said. They want to get out of their poverty. This was crazy but I knew what she meant. Her life was without a purpose. Caring for Merxplas gave her the illusion of a purpose. When I told her how much she helped us, she became hysterical. 'I hate Merxplas,' she cried. 'It shook me up, showed me how shallow was my peace of mind.' She leaned her forehead against the wall, the hat with that damned veil had fallen off, her groomed hair tousled into wild strains, her manicured fingers clawed the cement. Her shoulders were bowed and trembling, she broke into uncontrolled sobs. I could see the wild tomboy behind the masked society lady, the

woman behind the sphinx. I took her in my arms and told her so. We kissed. It was
madness, I can't explain it."

How well I understood!

"It was inexcusable," Benedikt continued. "We talked about running away together,
to a remote island where we could start a new life. Romantic insanity, but you know, for
a short moment, I believed it! We were literally saved by the bell. Faintly from above,
through all that cement, we heard the dinner bell and we were back in that bare,
monastic cell, filled with sacks of potatoes and boxes of dried herring. Helen snapped
open her bag, inspected herself in her mirror, restored her hat, her hair, her societal
war paint, and wandered off to the door, with little-girl steps. Just before leaving the
room, she turned, looked at me with her deep gazelle eyes, lifted herself on tiptoe and
kissed me on the cheek."

He forced a laugh. "And now I am supposed to go to her and ask for money. Instead
of the South Sea island, busfare." Barely audible he added, "I'm scared."

6.

Two days of freedom in Brussels. On the dogcatcher I was caught in the jittery
excitement of the first furlough but when we arrived at the Committee I felt forsaken,
overwhelmed by spasms of self-pity. Almost everyone else was welcomed by a friend,
a mother, a wife, a sweetheart. Laughter exploded all about me, joyful tears,
embraces, a chatter of voices breaking up in twosomes. The flock of arrivals melted
away, leaving only half a dozen lonely hearts behind.

I was grateful when Dr. Siebenschein approached me, unexpectedly cheerful, eyes
aflutter with good news. "We have a new director for our department of emigration. I
want you to meet Mademoiselle De Vries. She'll secure visas. You will want to write
about her in your newsletter."

Mademoiselle De Vries was a tall, sharp-featured woman, lean, hard, flat-chested,
with the charm of an army seargent. She reminded me of the wallflower girls in
dancing school, far removed from the blonde creampuffs of my story heroines. In spite
of her low rating on the femininity scale she was surrounded by a covey of men,
including Klingenberg, dewlaps wobbling, bending over, kissing her hand.
Wallflowers with visas in their pockets had irresistible allure in Brussels, 1939.

The trouble was she didn't have any visas in her pocket or anywhere else, as far as I
could find out. Dr. Siebenschein introduced me as the Merxplas reporter. She talked
vaguely about entry possibilities in the Belgian Congo and in a country Ruanda Urundi
which I must have missed in my geography lessons. I asked her about the Latin
American countries, and she said she was working on them. How about the prohibitive
demands of the American consul in Antwerp? She was working on that, too. I
mentioned several countries that were rumored as possibilities — Haiti, Cuba,
Panama, Cameroon, Angola? She was working on them all.

When I left, it was Max Hutt who was kissing her hand, telling her about his physical
training that made him ready for any heavy work. Pudgy Otto Einhorn detailed his
carpenter qualifications. Four others sat in a corner filling out forms.

7.

Life repeats itself, sometimes with dramatic variations. I left the 'emigration
department' in the same bleak mood I had left the American consulate a month ago.

And the first person I saw was Karla Berman. But in contrast to last time, she was furiously pacing up and down the room where the arrivals had met their welcoming friends. She wore a flowery crepe de Chine dress under a flapping coat, loop earrings jingling, and a torrent of black locks were swooping down from under a tiny velvet hat.

She turned to me, her ebony eyes flashing. "Where's Ted?"

I said he had been on the transport but she didn't listen. "I was a few minutes late," she stormed, "and he was gone. Probably speaking to someone about enemas and anti-syphilis pills. He doesn't give a damn about me. He doesn't need me. He needs his hospital. Louis needs *me*. I wasn't going to tell Ted but I will."

I tried to speak to her calmly, reasonably, but I was distracted by her bouncy curves, her pouty lips, her stamping feet, her fruity smell. I finally got her to sit down. I pleaded with her not to spoil this weekend for Berman, give herself time to sort things out. We didn't mention our last meeting but it never left my mind. My guilt made me preachy. I said things that were contrary to all of my past experiences. Perhaps for the first time in my life I glimpsed what was relevant — I spoke of the triviality of luxuries, of possessions, of sex. I suspect what I really spoke about was the triviality of the world of my short stories. I used Benedikt's terms: community, connectedness, belonging. She belonged to Berman, not to Pluvier.

I must have been convincing because she sat quietly, contemplating the hands in her lap. "What can I tell him?" she said in quiet desperation. "I no longer live with Susi, I have my own apartment, something I could never afford."

We concocted a story. She was to tell him that they would want Susi to have privacy with Willy, and that they, the Bermans, would take a room in a cheap hotel. For me, it was an exercise in fiction. To her it was a lie buying time.

We checked with Dr. Siebenschein about Berman. The attorney slapped his forehead. "Heavens," he apologized to Karla. "I forgot all about it. Dr. Berman went to the Zionist organization, just around the corner. He asked me to tell you to wait."

Just then Berman walked in. His face brightened when he saw Karla and gave her a bear hug. He stepped back, holding her hands, looking at her admiringly. "You have a new dress, a new coat, earrings?"

"The ladies from the auxiliary gave them to me," she lied. I thought I noticed a gleam of pleasure in her eyes. She was glad he'd noticed.

8.

The Committee had arranged hospitality for the few of us who didn't have friends or relatives in Brussels. In my pocket I carried the address of Michelle and Robert Bidou who expected me for dinner at six. It was not quite two. I strolled the streets, clutching a paperbag with my pajamas, toothbrush, and shaving equipment. I should have felt good, free for two days, a few francs in my wallet, ready for any adventure waiting around the corner. But I felt blah. As so often, I saw myself as a character in one of my short stories, but this time I was not the author who chose events to happen; I was being written by a noncaring Author who directed a plot that was out of my control. I was a stranger in a strange world, the surprises around the corner were threatening. The streets were bustling, but my mind was not on the restaurant sitters and window shoppers, the men in business suits, the pretty girls, the school children marching behind their teachers, the women bargaining with street vendors, the oldsters drawing on their pipes. My thoughts were with Herbert Waniek selling stamps and candy bars from a hole in the wall, who had the good sense to stay in camp because, like myself, he had no one in Brussels. I thought of Fred Glogau who had lost his only friend and couldn't understand why; of Richard Berliner who sought escape in a world of imagined Hollywood successes; and of embittered, gnomed Peter Kraus who taunted me with suffering from 'terminal optimism'.

It was a springy winter day, with clotted clouds blown across the sky, and stretches of sunshine. The neighborhood around *La Grand Place* was a large outdoor smorgasborg, with vendors hustling mussels, clams, shrimps, lobsters, oysters, and all sorts of fish. I bought a napkinful of crabs, not because I was hungry but because the pain in my stomach eased when I filled it. I bought a picture postcard of Brussels and wrote to my parents about my glorious vacation, the new emigration lady at the Committee, and my feeling great.

I passed the movie house where I had spent my first exhilarating evening in Belgium. They still played *Snow White and the Seven Dwarfs*. I bought a ticket and went in. But the colors, the music had lost their magic. The witch was real, the prince a fairytale. Another lie.

The Bidous lived near the Parc Royale. I walked the darkening streets, following my map. They lived in an ash-colored, two-story house behind a little front yard. The iron gate was open. I rang the bell at the wooden door with a brass plate saying, *Robert Bidou, Dentiste.*

A wispy woman with a doll mouth and long hair streaming down over her laced blouse opened the door, flashing a toothy smile. "You must be the refugee from the camp what's-its-name. I'm Michelle Bidou. Come in, we have a few friends over, you must tell us all about it."

The living room was a clutter of doily-covered little tables, knicknack-filled vitrines, potted plants, wall-hangings of needlework, brocaded cushions, and petit-points. The host, a hunched, ponderous man with a hooked beak, introduced me to three other couples sitting on a sofa and in arm chairs, holding wine glasses in one hand, cigarettes in the other.

"These are horrid stories we hear about this slob Hitler," Monsieur Bidou said. "What's he up to?"

Their attention span was short. Soon they were chattering in rapid French among each other, bubbling with laughter, noisy small talk, remembering me from time to time, asking questions with feigned sympathy. I don't remember much of the evening, except my dwindling hope that these samaritans-of-one-night might in some way help me.

The next morning, as promised, I visited the Benedikts. He sat on the only chair at a tiny table, a towel tucked at the front of his shirt, a cup of warm water before him, shaving. The attic room had no ceiling, the wall sloped from the floor 45-degrees upwards, cutting the room diagonally in half. A small window in the slanted wall allowed a bit of light.

Natascha boiled tea on a gas burner. Washlines crossed the room. On the iron cot sat Herbert Blei, Benedikt's schoolmate, one of the envied emigrants who had been allowed to stay in Brussels with his young wife.

"You don't know how lucky you are," Benedikt said, scraping at his chin. "Even in this rabbit hole, where water drips on you from your own shirts. Your attic is your castle. You can shave with warm water. Go to bed and get up when you feel like it. Take a walk without filling out a petition. Life has treasures you appreciate only after you've lost them."

Blei kept quiet. "Tea is ready," Natascha emerged from under a piece of drying underwear. "Get your shaving stuff off the table, Jack. The mess you made! "

Benedikt removed his soap and brush. "See how I am treated, Berti? In Merxplas I'm a trustee with a gold star, and here I'm just in the way."

"A man in an attic is a drip off a samovar." Natascha said. "Russian proverb."

"How do you handle the unfair sex in a mousehole, Berti?" Benedikt cleansed his razor under the sink. "You have experience."

Blei said in a strangled voice, "We're separating, Gretl and I."

Benedikt froze at the faucet. I knew they had been friends throughout high school and college.

"How is that possible?" He sat down on the cot, next to Blei. "Is it Gretl's fault? Or yours?"

Blei gestured vaguely toward the room. "This is at fault. This cage. This life. We're together all day long, and the day has a thousand irritations. I'm used to going to work. Now I sit home. Whatever you do costs money, every streetcar fare, every cup of coffee. These attics are the graveyards of marriage. A woman can be busy in such a room, cook, wash, make beds. The man feels useless. He *is* useless. He doesn't forgive his wife that she is now the more essential partner. It's idiotic, I know. But these idiocies wreck the marriage. And this slanted ceiling! Every time you sit up you bump your head. First you laugh about it, but the fiftieth time you go mad."

"But these are trifles."

"These trifles ruin a marriage. They turn you inside out, and bring out what's hidden. I've seen a Gretl I never knew and would have never known after fifty years of marriage in Frankfurt. She probably feels the same way about me."

I thought I noticed a furtive glance between Natascha and Benedikt. It could mean a hunch of fear: what about us? Benedikt placed a palm on his friend's knee. "Forgive me, Berti. But there is really nothing else? Nobody else?"

Blei shook his head. "Nothing like that. We'll remain friends. Officially, we'll even stay together."

"It will pass," Benedikt said, without conviction.

"No, we talked it all over. I'll still take Gretl with me to America. We have a common affidavit, but I was born in Germany, she in Poland. My number will come up soon, the Polish quota is taken up for years. As my wife she comes under my quota."

"Bureaucracy will save you," Benedikt said. "In America you'll be the breadwinner again."

"As specialist in German constitutional law? No, I'd have to go to college all over again. It's dishwasher for me."

"You can practice here," Natascha said. "Let's have lunch."

The lunch was subdued. Conversation to paper over tragedy.

Then Benedikt turned to Natascha, with the exaggerated mannerism of a business executive, "I'll have to attend to some camp matters. I told you. It's about getting money for the monthly visits."

"From Helen Pleienberg?"

"Her women's auxiliary. It's a sizeable sum."

"She'll know what to do."

It may have been my imagination but I thought there was stress in their voices.

"I had a sitting scheduled," Natascha said. "I meant to postpone it, but since you are busy anyway . . ."

"Natascha is painting portraits of Committee bigshots," Benedikt explained.

"Mostly their wives." Natascha was busy clearing away the dishes. "Where d'you think the money for the lamb chops came from?"

"See?" Blei smiled wanly. "They earn, we beg."

"The bus leaves at four," Benedikt said. "Shall I pick you up here or do we meet at the Committee?"

"Let's meet at the Committee," Natascha decided. "You may need a little time to convince the princess."

There was strain in their embrace. And unspoken words.

9.

Again I wandered through the streets of that unfamiliar city. I thought of Benedikt and Natascha, of Berman and Karla, of Kruger and Susi, and wondered if I would ever have a Natascha, a Karla, a Susi. For the first time in my life I thought of a wife, not a curvacious blonde with a trilly voice but a comrade like my mother was to my father. They had a home, it had been my home, too. Now it was gone. For me, there was no home, now or in the future. And I realized, with a grip of panic, that Merxplas, the camp for vagrants, was my home. The Benedikts, the Bermans, the Wanieks, Neumanns, Berbers, Klingenbergs were my family. Even Heino Wolf belonged to it.

My steps had led me to the Committee. It was still more than an hour before departure time. The rabbit warren of little rooms was crowded with refugees, some new and bewildered, some experienced in their new nonlife, picking up allowances, rumor-mongering, boasting of lost possessions, speculating visa possibilities — familiar stuff. Cecilia de Vries's office was besieged with hand-kissers and form-fillers. Dr. Siebenschein repeated his nervous warnings against German-speaking in the streets. A bespectacled, fretful woman leafed through lists and gave new arrivals addresses of cheap rooms for rent. One gruff and grumpy man actually envied me for having found a haven in Merxplas. Siebenschein told him they were working on establishing more camps, perhaps even for families. For the first time I felt misgiving that refugeedom was becoming a permanent state.

Gradually the returnees drifted in, accompanied by mothers with tear-filled eyes, quietly unhappy wives, and artificially cheerful friends. I found a relatively quiet corner and started writing in my notebook. I scribbled in a shorthand so hectic I can hardly decipher it today. I poured my choked heart on sheet after sheet — my hatred of the Nazis, my anger at the closed world, my fear of the future, my doubts, frustration, despair. I hardly noticed that the dogcatcher had arrived and the rooms were filled with returnees. I was relieved to see Berman, gaunt, square jawed, but Karla at his side. I tried to catch her eye but she seemed withdrawn into a cocoon of her own. But they were together, that's what counted! Natascha was here, scanning the arrivals for Benedikt. He came only a few minutes before the dogcatcher left. I was already in the van and watched them talk earnestly, heads close, hands on each other's shoulders. He climbed aboard at the last moment and I had no chance to speak to him.

We arrived at Merxplas just before the dinner bell. He carried his night things in an attache briefcase, mine were in the paper bag. We took them upstairs to the dorm.

"How did it go?" I asked.

"All right," he said, curtly. He sat down on his cot, gnawing at his underlip. I wanted to know, and sat next to him.

He looked at me with a hint of his old grin. "Helen didn't think it would be easy to get this steady stream of money from the auxiliary committee. Not so much because they couldn't raise it but because they're not too keen on having us around. But Helen had an idea to hook them. The ladies don't want us in Brussels but are curious about the camp. Helen suggested we arrange a Merxplas festival, show what we can do, performances, music, a show, nothing too serious. The auxiliary will sell tickets. Society people, invite the press. Hubert Pleienberg undoubtedly will make a speech. A festival will bring in money, solve our problems."

I had another question but he quickly added, "Talk to Neumann about the festival. He'll love it. Here's the dinner bell. Come on."

He never mentioned anything more of his meeting with Helen, and I never asked.

X. A Slap in the Face

1.

Benedikt was right: Siegfried Neumann's face lit up in neon lights when he heard about the "Merxplas Festival." But his illumination paled compared to the fireworks that exploded in Richard Berliner.

"Great!" he boomed. "Hot-cha-cha! We'll slay 'em. I'll put on a show the like of which these suckers have never seen! We'll do *Lear*. I did it in Hannover. Rave reviews all the way to Berlin."

"They want something light," Benedikt injected gently.

"*Twelfth Night*," Berliner enthused. "They've never forgotten my Malvolio in Stuttgart!"

"I did *Charly's Aunt* in a Vienna night club," Neumann suggested. "Funny as hell."

Our "theater group" was meeting with Benedikt in the library after dinner: Neumann, Jäger, Berber, Berliner, and I.

Berliner's contemptuous grimace demonstrated physical pain. "Listen," he said, "if this is to be Amateur Night, count me out."

"What the people in Brussels have in mind," Benedikt reported, "is a talent show. Light. Cabaret style."

"*Doktorchen* can do it." Jäger winked at me. He had taken to calling me "*Doktorchen*" — affectionate for "little doctor."

The word 'cabaret' made my brain cells churn and bubble. Berber's tall tales of "Kingdom Merxplas" flashed through my mind and I saw tempting possibilities.

"I could write a take-off on our life here," I burst out, surprised at my sudden enthusiasm.

"A satire!" Berliner flared up, looking at me with ebullient eyes. "Our own Aristophanes. I did the *Birds* in Munich. Sensational!"

"Would you do it?" Benedikt asked me.

I felt inexplicably pleased. To write a cabaret sketch for Merxplas seemed the most desirable thing in the world.

"This could be the center piece," Benedikt continued. "We'll look for other talents. Show them what we can do."

"You're grabbing the ass by the wrong tail," Berliner said. "If you ask for talents, four hundred dingbats will show up. Everyone who has ever committed a New Year's poem or sang at grandma's birthday, considers himself a poet or a singer. God forbid. First *we* have to decide the grand plan. Then we'll do the auditioning. We need a decent stage, floodlights, a curtain. Props, make-up, a decent piano . . ."

"Who's going to pay for all this?" Benedikt asked.

"The Committee, of course."

"The Committee wants to make money, not spend it."

"Every theater wants that, but it has to invest. You want us to hop around on four joined tables, lit up by two old oil lamps, without scenery, and instead of a curtain simply say, 'That's it, folks, show's over'? No, kids, to a ham show I'll never lend my name."

It took a lot of convincing until the old man saw the point of our festival: to show what we had been able to accomplish. Our carpentry class was to build the stage, our electrician students install the lighting, our tailoring trainees sew the costumes. Berliner voiced objections at every step. There was something touching about his utter lack of comprehension. He spoke of printed programs with ads from Belgian businesses, a buffet during intermission, of decorating the dayroom with potted plants "as a winter garden." When we wrestled him down to reality, we blocked out the program in broad outlines. My sketch was to be the centerpiece. Berber's dancing, Neumann's comic, Jäger's accordion playing, and talents still to be discovered all would be used. In the midst of our planning the night bell sounded.

"*Gott im Himmel!*" Berliner grumped. "Fine rehearsals we'll have if those sieve-brained bureaucrats will interrupt every moment with their goddamned dingdongs. We'll have to get permission to stay up later. And be sure we get strong black coffee and cigarettes at all times."

To Berliner, it was a matter of course that the laws of prison and emigration would be suspended for the laws of theater.

2.

During the next three weeks we enjoyed an onslaught of theatromania. I suspect that at the start most inmates were only vaguely aware of the preparations for the Great Event set for Sunday, March 5. But the pebble of our thespian enthusiasm drew ever-wider circles. Berliner pronounced himself the producer-director-dramaturgist and demanded top billing on the marquee. Since we would never have anything resembling a marquee his wish was generously granted. He set up his director's office in a corner of the library. Here he spent all his time after his dwindling English class to audition, discover talents, engage, "contract." "Pick up your advance at the camp treasury," was his steady joke to those he "hired." He held story conferences with me, discussed cast problems with Berber who was to be the star of the show, rehearsed with Franzl Jäger whom he anointed musical director, and instructed Hermi Schaub, the young and talented cartoonist, who was to paint the backdrops. Berliner, in his threadbare three-piece suit, monocle clamped over his hollow right eye, smoking furiously his twisted, self-made cigarettes, measured the space for the stage in the dayroom of Pavilion B, decided the placing of scenery and lighting, negotiated with the teachers of the retraining classes about building the stage and props, installing the lighting, and sewing the costumes. Pacing furiously back and forth, poking the air with a nicotine-tinted forefinger, he dictated letters to the Committee with monstrous demands, most of which were quietly censored by Benedikt and me. He even gained the amused cooperation of Heino Wolf and his police gang to allow exceptions from the strictly enforced camp rules, to accommodate our histrionic enterprise.

I, too, caught the festival bug. I don't remember having ever been as eager to write anything, before or after, as I was concocting the little sketch that was to be the centerpiece of the production, an opera parody about the Kingdom Merxplas and its caricatured citizens. Franzl Jäger joined Berber and me in the sickroom to toss about ideas, breaking out in bits of arias, trying out dance steps, cheering an idea, roaring about a gag. Berman would try to shoo us away with a line mockingly repeated to his face whenever he showed up: "Shush, you guys. A hospital is no theater."

Our spirits were lifted by the unexpected response to Berliner's requests. The women's auxiliary sent used electrical equipment, poster paint and brushes, materials for costumes, and even tattered bits and pieces of fur which Oskar Pitman declared good enough to fashion into a stole. He was a crude and growly man with frizzy hair and mustache who had owned a fur store on Vienna's most elegant shopping street and now taught a furrier retraining course — so far with imitation pieces. Pitman suggested we have a raffle, with his stole as first prize, a suggestion welcomed by all except Berliner who scorned it as "stooping to carnival hoopla." The most welcome gift was an upright piano so out of tune that Franzl Jäger suspected it came from the archeological museum. The next morning a shy little bookkeeper-type approached me, a wire-rimmed pincenez hanging from his neck on a black cord, and said apologetically that in his youth he had wanted to become a concert pianist and he knew how to tune a piano. He worked on it in the dayroom of Pavilion B, during our free time after dinner, undaunted by the chattering of 300 voices and the hammering of the crew setting up the stage. Four days later he reported his work done — a changed man, self-assured and beaming. Music director Jäger declared the piano good enough to play a Beethoven concerto on, and the frustrated concert pianist, whose name was Berthold Stern, volunteered to do just that. We sent him to Papa Berliner for auditioning, who declared him "a rare find in this human pigsty" and "engaged" Stern to open the show with the Egmont overture.

(This assignment gave Stern the idea to plan his future as a piano tuner rather than a bookkeeper, and he started teaching a piano-tuning course in the camp.)

Meanwhile my opera was taking shape, and we rehearsed between dinner and bedtime. It was called "The Golden Stars," and showed the future Kingdom Merxplas, the citizenry grown old, ruled by pompous King Ernest, the Magnificent, a caricature of Ernst Holländer, and his bizarre cabinet of gold-star bearers including the police chief, a lampoon on Heino Wolf. The kingdom was divinely protected by a benevolent fairy godmother in mimicry of Helen Pleienberg. The opera featured arias of longing for the jungles of the Amazon, a nostalgic duet about the "good old times" of 1939, and a sextet of floor washers, all former attorneys, college professors, and bank directors. At the happy ending two angels appeared scattering oversea visas among the grateful Merxplasians.

We used a lot of Offenbach and popular arias by Verdi, Mozart, and Wagner. Neumann as King Ernest, and Berber as the fairy godmother Helena, contributed new gags at almost every rehearsal, and Berthold Stern soon got into the spirit and surprised us with musical tomfoolery. Often the rehearsals got so out of hand that Berliner blew up, cursed, held his head in both hands, and screamed that he would not waste his time with this bunch of dilettantes. He found the most colorful invectives for us which I noted in my diary and which translate roughly as balloonheads, mush-tongued dodos, prunewits, flea-witted muttonheads, and wrinkled-assed nincompoops. His favorite explosive was the equally hard-to-translate "go and shovel your own shit," which he hissed into our faces before he stormed out of the room. But, as we knew, he soon returned to "give us another chance."

Actually we realized that the old man was not suited to direct a cabaret piece, and Berber very tactfully took over, leaving Berliner the illusion that he was in full charge. We had impromptu rehearsals, without Berliner, in the sickroom, especially during the free hour before lunch. While Berber and I attended to the patients, actors would clump into the room and try out snatches of scenes with new twists. Berman would go through his this-is-a-hospital-and-not-a-theater routine but since no one was seriously sick at the time, he let us clown before the patients, while Berber assured him that "humor was a better medicine than an enema." In the sickroom Berber also rehearsed a "ballet" scene he invented and which was to be a high point of my opera. He selected six young men who were made up as old, bent, and limping on crutches, having spent 50 years in Merxplas. After creeping along painfully they suddenly threw off their crutches and broke in a wild, high-kicking dance. It was amazing to see how Berber was able to turn these stiff, clumsy boys into something resembling a ballet. They clung in enthusiastic admiration to Berber and were willing to practice the same steps over and over again.

3.

A few days before the Festival Berman entered the sick room and stood a few moments watching the ongoing rehearsal with amused resignation.

"When you possibly can spare a moment from being Molière," he told me, "step into my office. I now have a gastroscope."

His "office" was a cubicle next to the sickroom where he examined patients, and sometimes, when one of the patients was seriously sick, slept at night on a folding cot. Occasionally Berber or I slept on that cot, a notable exception from the camp rules granted by Vandenheuvel. The room smelled of disinfectants and camomile. I knew every pill box on the shelf but now, for the first time, I was the patient. Berman and I sat on the only two chairs. We had often talked about my stomach trouble but now he took my case history officially. The more we talked the grimmer he looked. I tried to cheer him and myself by saying that for the past two weeks I had felt fine. He noted that down, nodded, and said, "This is not going to be pleasant but I'll have to give you a gastroscopy."

'Not going to be pleasant' turned out to be a painful understatement. The gastroscope consisted of a thin hose which I had to swallow. I gagged, gasped for air, retched, and to my amazement was actually able to get the tube down my throat and into my stomach. Berman peered through it for what seemed to be an excruciating eternity. He finally retrieved the thing and the world returned to normal, with air to breathe, camomile to smell. Through the door came the sound of my parody of Tannhäuser's Evening Star which, in translation of the original German, would go like, "Oh, thou, resplendent Golden Star," and I knew I was back in Merxplas where we made fun of the trustees with their golden stars.

"Well," Berman said, jaw clamped. "I was hoping it wouldn't be, but it is. You've got an ulcer. Not bleeding but bad enough. We'll have to get you out of here fast."

"But not before the show," I heard myself reply, and he broke into a mirthless laugh.

"If I'd my say, tomorrow. But the red tape won't unwind so fast. No one was yet released from this dungeon without a one-way ticket out of Belgium. I'll go to Pluvier if necessary. The food here would kill you. You'll have to go on a milk diet. One or two weeks won't make a difference. Meanwhile, no coffee, no candy bars. Luckily, you don't smoke. Don't eat much at meal time and keep some of the food for in-between snacks. Bread, potatoes, even if you have to eat them cold. Keep on writing your show. Throw yourself into it, it's your best medicine right now. But after it's over, out you go, and it's baby food for you!"

That night, on my cot, my brain was awhirl with a litter of messed-up thoughts. To survive in that savage dog-eat-dog world out there, I had to be well. For the first time I faced the possibility of dying, not merely thinking about it but experiencing it in my imagination. These were not other people dying, it was me, ME! Here was the end, a big black Nothing, and I was overcome by horror. I listened to the pounding of my heart blending into the snores and strangled nightmare groans of my comrades-in-fate, and after a while the panic subsided.

4.

March 5, 1939. The first private cars arrived. The grassy plot between the two pavilions had been assigned as parking lot. A platinum haze lay over the heath, the sun was an orange someone had cut from a magazine and pasted in the sky. Where unshaven figures in blue work clothes used to lug buckets of coal, shrub flagstones, and peel potatoes, glittering women with ceramic complexions and complacent men with boomy laughs wandered through the massive brick buildings as through a museum. For one day the inmates had changed back into the persons they had been before their disfranchisement: Klingenberg into the professor, Kellner into the bank vice-president, Gal into the man of the world. They wore their best, and often only, suit. Only Holländer had not changed back into his original insignificance. He flaunted his mastery over the vagabond state marching around in a Napoleonic pose. It struck me how close he came to his parody in my opera.

The rooms sparkled of cleanliness. The dayrooms were comfortably heated and Hermi Schaub had decorated the bare walls with caricatures of life in Merxplas. The barred windows were discretely covered with curtains, the cots in the dormitories were lined up like a piano keyboard, the tables in the dining hall set in advance, and Waniek's canteen displayed its chocolate bars. The arts-and-crafts course had supplied signs and guideposts, and my bulletin board found much attention. I overheard two chunky men looking at the list showing the stand of our chess tournament.

"They play chess," one of them said. "When do *we* have time for things like that?"

The library contained our exhibit. Every retraining class displayed its products: the cobblers a pair of boots; the tailors an overcoat; the furriers the stole to be raffled off; the arts-and-crafts workshop copper figures, woven fabrics, and talisman dolls for cars; the bakers a cake in the form of a Merxplas pavilion. Also available for sightseeing was the stage where everything from the props to the costumes and electrical equipment was done in our workshops.

The dogcatcher had brought forty wives who could afford the trip. Lucille Clairmont arrived from Turnhout in her father's old car. Some of the refugees working at the Committee had come in cars of our Belgian benefactors. Mousy Siebenschein made his first appearance at the camp, and Cecilia de Vries marched through the halls, large-boned and square-jawed, surrounded by visa-hungry men who attached themselves to her like a swarm of bees to their queen. Three reporters poked into corners and popped flashlights. Lunch was served in two shifts, one for the inmates and one for the guests. Lobositz had dipped deep into our meager supplies to prepare leek soup, herring filet with potato pancake, and squares of Viennese chocolate cake.

After lunch the performance was planned, and stage fever was rampant behind the curtain we had actually been able to obtain. Berliner, busy as a hummingbird, bustled about scattering last-minute instructions, encouragements, and invectives. In his rich theatralical voice he spoke of "snowing these yahoos," of rave reviews, and going on tour throughout Belgium. In this chaos of primping, chattering, and scrambling men I found myself on the sidelines. My job was done, and I vaguely worried how the Committee people would take our burlesquing them.

Willy Kruger ran up to me, wide-eyed, hands aflutter. He dragged me to the side of the stage where we could look at the audience. The tables had been taken out and the large hall was filled with rows of benches. The guests sat in front, our own people farther back. The air was filled with the hum of the waiting audience. Kruger, with a jerk of his chin, pointed to the left side of the audience. There, in the first row, sat Karla Berman next to Louis Pluvier.

"Does Berman know?" Kruger asked.

"I don't think so," I stammered. "Not really. Maybe he guessed."

"How could she!" Kruger exploded. "She looks radiant. Happy. What does she want to prove?"

"Has Berman seen them?" I asked.

"Someone broke a finger. He's in his office applying a splint."

At this moment Franzl Jäger stepped before the curtain and welcomed the visitors. He was master of ceremony. Nothing ever fazed him. He had an inborn, playful humor and always remained his natural, witty self. He didn't want any help in writing his material, nor did he need it. He introduced Berthold Stein who opened the show with Beethoven's Egmont overture, played by heart. The program balanced comedy with solemnity, we took care to avoid excesses in either direction. Peter Kraus limped onto the stage and sang his sad ballad of the Jewish mother whose child was taken from her. Franzl Jäger followed with a take-off on a radio news broadcast about Merxplas. Berber staged a Spanish tavern scene with various inmates singing, playing the violin, piano, and harmonica, concluding with a dance with castagnettes performed by Berber and his group of youngsters. Jäger and Neumann did a short farce, and Berber performed a serious solo dance, "The Emigrant," to the tune of Rachmaninoff. When the curtain went up, he stood on the dark stage, spotlighted by a single beam. He wore only a torn shirt and pants. He moved slowly, as in a dream, as if he still could not comprehend what had happened to him. He tried to escape in different directions but everywhere he was repulsed by unseen hands. His flight became increasingly hectic, the barriers closed in, his efforts to escape grew more and more desperate. With discheveled hair falling over his moist forehead, with gaping shirt and the crazed look of a hunted animal he tried in a last attempt to break out his trap, but to no avail. Exhausted, hunted to death, he collapsed.

The centerpiece was the opera about Kingdom Merxplas. I watched the performance from the wing, with Berliner at my side who followed every move of the actors with repressed shouts of enthusiasm, gestures of annoyance, and strangled sounds of despair. When the angels sent by fairy godmother Helena came out with their huge cornucopias scattering visas all over the stage to the tune of the Blue Danube Waltz, there was applause and cheering. The actors took their bows. Suddenly Berliner grabbed my hand and dragged me across the stage, pushing everyone aside and taking an elegant bow. He then pointed to me, and it was music to my ears to hear the applause swell to a crescendo. I had always had fantasies of bow-taking at the world premiere of my play at the Vienna Burgtheater. This was a far cry from it, but I must admit this moment was a high point of my life.

5.

The benches were quickly pushed against the walls, and our dance band, led by Jäger's accordion, occupied the stage. A bee line formed to Cecilia de Vries. She had taken off her glasses and wore a feminine chiffon dress but still looked like a top sergeant dancing with privates. The huge dance floor of the dayroom filled slowly with inmates who had partners — Gal and Lucille, Benedikt and Natascha, Kruger and

Susi. Even Holländer clumsily trotted about with his plump spouse when he saw reporters popping their flashbulbs. Very few of the invited guests participated in the dance. In fact, many went to their cars and left. A handful stopped by me and congratulated me on my skit. Trite phrases, tinsel smiles, routine handshakes, but I felt on top of a mountain. I was Someone and Useful.

Then my heart did a somersault. I spotted Berman among the onlookers. He stared across the dance floor, his jaw muscles working. Pluvier was dancing with Karla, cheek to cheek. I quickly walked over to him and put my hand on his arm. He paid no heed and strode across the floor with a determined, hard-as-steel look.

He stopped at Pluvier and Karla, and said coldly, "Mind if I dance with my wife?"

Pluvier stopped, still holding Karla in dance position. "Your wife decides for herself with whom she wishes to dance," he chirped with his boyish voice.

Berman pulled her from Pluvier's grip. "Karla," he pleaded. "Be sensible."

"I don't want to be sensible," she exploded, with a furious toss of her glissening black hair. "And I don't want to lie any longer."

Berman swayed on his feet, hit by every one of the battering words she hurled at him. "Always thinking! Examining! Diagnosing! Considering! Weighing! Never *living!*" Suddenly her face softened. She looked vulnerable, defenseless. "I want to live, Teddy!"

"We'll live, Karla," he said gently. "The Zionists in Brussels will get us to Palestine."

"A fine life you will have in your Palestine." Pluvier's voice curdled with irony. "Karla needs comfort, beautiful things, luxuries . . ."

"Karla has never craved luxury. You made her, you and your damned money."

"Money is damned only by those who don't have it. Karla is not cut out to be a poor man's wife. Emigration is a test for marriage."

"Emigration is a killer of marriage!" Berman spit out the words, with the quick, sharp movements of a creature attacked. Other couples had stopped dancing and watched the scene while I stood by, helplessly.

"Look, Teddy," Karla said with a quick, fragile smile. "You have your work. Your faith in Palestine. You don't need me. Louis needs me. If you say you need me, I'll stay with you."

I could feel Berman's smoldering fury. His body stiffened, his face was deeply lined in bitter resignation. "Go," he said tonelessly. "I don't need you."

"You see," Pluvier took possession of Karla like a trophy. "He doesn't need you." Then jovially to Berman: "Listen, I have banking connections in London. If your heart lies with Palestine I'll raise the deposit for your immigration visa, and we will all be happy."

Berman leaped forward and slapped Pluvier's face. In the scramble that followed, Heino Wolf shouldered his way through the cluster of onlookers and grabbed Berman's arm. "Take it easy, doc."

"That's what you get for getting involved with refugees," Pluvier shouted. "I spent a fortune for this camp. This clown asked me for it as if his life depended on it. And now he slaps me!"

A reporter took a picture. "That's how they are, the Jews," he remarked.

René Dierx, the main guard, stepped in and took Berman from Wolf. "Behave yourself," he told Berman. "Remember you are a guest in our country."

"In which the host steals my wife! Who thinks his money gives him the right to break up a marriage."

"Money has nothing to do with Karla's decision," Pluvier said blithely.   "And being a Jew nothing with the slap," Berman countered.

"Come on" Dierx said sternly. "We've already called the police."

Berman shook off the guard's hand from his arm. "So *I* get arrested, and not the adulterer?" A wild desperate look came over his face. For a moment I was afraid he would throw himself onto Dierx.

"Be sensible," Karla said.

Berman slackened like a puppet whose string was cut. He did not resist when Dierx took him away. I thought of Judge Stein. Here was a man who had lost his home, his wife, and his rights.

6.

The slapping incident was blown out of all proportions. The Belgian press picked it up and made the slap of a husband at his wife's lover into a slap of the refugees at their host country. Dormant anti-Semitism and anti-German feelings emerged from under the veneer of civilized tolerance. Editorials called for "setting an example," for returning the criminal to Germany. We held an emergency meeting of the trustees to discuss what we could do. Suggestions ranged from writing letters to the major newspapers to sending petitions to the chief of police, writing to Louis Pluvier's father who was a member of parliament, even to the King.

"A lot of good this will do," remarked Wolf, his lips curled in a derisive smirk.

"What would *you* do?" someone challenged.

"Act, not talk," Wolf said.

"For instance?" Neidhart asked. "Hunger strike?"

"Why not?"

We called a general meeting. The hunger strike was rejected but I was surprised that almost one hundred inmates voted for it, mostly those who had come with the early transports and had taken part in the forming of the community. Finally we decided to send Benedikt to Helen Pleienberg, to ask her intervention. Vandenheuvel, who proved to be fair and even sympathetic, granted the furlough.

Benedikt looked uncomfortable when he left, and downright depressed when he returned. I could tell by his contorted face, his lifeless eyes that his mission had been a failure. Worse: Berman had been shipped back to Aachen that very day!

A shroud of despair settled over the camp. All we had hoped and worked for in our Festival had been dashed and turned into dejection. Rumors spread like epidemics — the Committee would abandon us, the police would take over the camp, we would all be returned to Germany. Neidhart dictated a calming "editorial" for my newsletter, of not much avail. Manic irritability alternated with waves of depression. Many of the men became physically sick, and Kruger, even with the help of Robert Klimt, our pharmacist, could not handle the beleaguered hospital. I myself felt the fireball in my stomach and had specters of dying.

The next day a rumor floated through the camp which turned out to be true: Heino Wolf had disappeared! Had he gone into hiding? Should we do the same thing? I asked Weinkraut if he knew what happened. He just grinned his lopsided smirk.

7.

Just when it appeared that even the flimsy security underpinning of the camp was yanked from under our feet, I received a letter from Max. The British were now allowing prospective immigrants to the United States, who had an affidavit and 100 English pounds, to come to England and await their quota number there. Max and I had earned that amount of money by selling our short stories. He enclosed an application form for my British entry visa. I was to send it to the Bloomsbury House in London, the German Jewish Aid Committee, who would take the necessary steps. Once in England, I would simply   wait for my American quota number to mature. The American consul in London made no extra demands.

This was life-saving news. I sent off my application immediately. And yet I felt an inexplicable sadness at the thought of leaving the camp. I confided in only one man, Benedikt. He had been dejected since Berman's deportation, but when he heard my news he burbled and spluttered as in old times. He spoke of all of us getting out eventually, of new lives somewhere, some time. His cascade of optimism was contageous but when I went to the sickroom again, and saw Berber, that great artist, changing sheets for a skeleton of a patient, all the sadness flooded back. We had lost two of our best, Judge Stein and Dr. Berman. Wolf had abandonned us, Benedikt was hiding his ordeal. He never even hinted at his predicament with Helen, and his rapport with Natascha seemed strained. Here were 600 human beings, their lives smashed, caught in a trap that gave them temporary shelter, their pain made a little more bearable by sharing.

The next few days crept by. I busied myself in the sickroom where Kruger and Klimt had their hands full. Berman's calm authority was badly missed. On the fourth day Ludwig Sommer, the Hermes of the camp, rushed into the sickroom, excitement all over his horsy face. He usually specialized in horror stories (which mostly turned out to be true) but this time his news was good: Wolf was back!

Berber and I bombarded him with questions but Sommer knew no more. Wolf had limped in, disheveled and tightlipped. He was wearing the old clothes in which he had come to the camp. They were torn and bloody, Sommer reported, before scuttling out again to spread the word.

We didn't have to wait long to have Sommer's report confirmed. Wolf himself hobbled into the little doctor's office, in his camp uniform, the golden star on his beret.

"I hurt my leg, doc," he told Kruger. "See what you can do."

Kruger pulled up the right leg of Wolf's pants. "That's a gunshot."

"Good diagnosis, doc. In and out. Not much damage done. I did first aid with rags from my underpants. Stopped the bleeding "

"What happened?"

"A little disagreement."

"With whom?"

"Listen, doc." Wolf's voice become impatient. "Do your Hippocrates and save my life, will you? And spare me the third degree."

I had a dozen questions I didn't ask while I helped Kruger disinfect the two wounds. If they hurt, Wolf didn't let on.

Neither would he or any of his gang say more. The rumor mill worked overtime but no one knew anything. Even Sommer admitted defeat.

"Probably did a little unfinished smuggling," he guessed.

My own futile guesswork was interrupted by a letter from the London Bloomsbury House. Enclosed was a visa application card which I was to present, together with my passport, to the British Consul in Antwerp.

8.

This time everything went smoothly. I received a one-day leave from Vandenheuvel, and the visa from the British consulate. When I returned to the camp, I knew it was for the last time. I was superbly happy and unaccountably sad. The word had spread, and I encountered genuine affection, as well as envy, among the well-wishers. And I discovered genuine grief as well as guilt in myself.

One of the first to approach me was a tittering Sommer. He clapped his hand to his cheek. "Oi, am I embarrassed," he shouted in self-mockery. "I didn't know about the British transit visa. I have an affidavit and easily can raise the hundred pounds. I'll apply today."

I shook scores of hands, received dozens of shoulder claps, saw brave smiles, and tear-filled eyes. I felt my throat tighten many times.

After dinner which was to be my last, Wolf came by. "Let's take a walk," he grunted out of the corner of his mouth. I followed him to the washroom in Pavilion B which was locked at the time. Wolf fiddled with the lock for a moment and the door opened. This would have been the ideal place to write my stories in peace if I had Wolf's skills.

He leaned against the trough-like sink. "Listen, you go to Brussels?"

I nodded uneasily, wondering what spurious business he had in store for me.

"You know how to get in touch with Karla Berman?"

This took me by surprise. "Susi Kruger might know," I said.

"Good." he thrust his hand in his pocket and dug out a crumpled piece of paper. He handed it to me. "See that she gets this."

I glanced at the paper. It contained a penciled address. I looked at Wolf for an explanation.

"That's where she can find the doc," Wolf said.

"Berman?"

Wolf nodded, enjoying my consternation.

."But how . . ." I started but he cut me short.

"He's there," he stated. "Tell her he NEEDS her." He spoke the word in capital letters. "It's in Holland, just over the border. No trick to get there from Belgium. If she needs help . . ." he grabbed the note out of my hand and scribbled on it. "Here is someone who'll help her."

"But how did he get there? And how do you know?"

He grinned, and things began to fall into place.

"You mean . . ."

His grin broadened. "The doc is a pal. When Jonatai was sick he saved his life. He saved a lot of lives. When a pal is in trouble you do something. All you yo-yos do is talk. Write petitions."

"What did you do? He was deported. You didn't go to Germany to get him?"

"That's where he was, wasn't he? It's not hard to get *into* Germany."

"Where did you find him?"

"You got three guesses."

"In prison?"

"Boy, you're a genius."

"How did you get him out?"

"I know a lot of bentnoses everywhere."

I had heard about his smuggler past. Perhaps he had accomplices in the Aachen police. Perhaps he used force. I had visions of knocked-down guards, ropes, gags. I pointed at his leg. "Is that how you got this?"

"Nah," he said. "I know my way around the Belgian border. But the doc wouldn't be safe in Belgium. I had to get him into Holland. That's where I had a bit of trouble."

He wouldn't tell me more. I had to fill in the gaps in my imagination. I had many questions. How did he get out of Merxplas? No sweat, he said, there was no wall around the camp, was there? "A noble experiment in prison reform," he added, sarcastically. When I inquired foolishly if he had asked Vandenheuvel, he laughed.

"Ask, and it shall be forbidden to you," he misquoted the Scriptures. He slapped his thigh and abruptly ended our talk. "You just see that Karla gets the message." He moved close to me and squinted at me. "And no word to anyone, hear?"

We left the washroom. My head was full of unanswerable questions. How did he do it? Find Berman in an Aachen prison, free him, take him across the border to Belgium, then across the Dutch border, leave Berman with a friend, and return to Merxplas? Every question raised a legion of others. If Wolf had all these connections, why had he and his gang allowed themselves to be taken to Merxplas, and why did they stay here? Was it a hide-out? Did they plan anything in the camp? I remembered their attempt to smuggle in prostitutes with the first women's visits. But the inmates of Merxplas were unlikely victims of any money-making scheme. Was Merxplas the base of some outside strikes? I let my fantasy roam but found no answer credible even in a short story. Wolf's escapade to Aachen was beyond belief. I never found the answer, only a hint — much later.

9.

It borders on sacrilege to compare my farewell from Vienna and my parents with the farewell from my comrades in Merxplas with whom I had shared life for less than half a year. When I sat in the bus taking me to Brussels, the red brick buildings of Merxplas flying by, scraps of scenes flashed numbly through my mind: Berber's silent hug; Waniek's tinsely smile; Berliner's Shakespearean good-bye; Fred Glogau's waiflike helplessness; Neidhart's slap of camaraderie; Neumann's bobbing Adam's apple; Sommer's ponderous affection; Franzl Jäger's mock dramatics; Willy Kruger fluttering wave; Wolf's wink of conspiracy; Klingenberg's unctuous prayerlike mumble; and — more intense than anything — Benedikts firm handclasp and the bonding of our eyes. I didn't want it to be true but I knew I would not see any of them, ever.

My final task in Brussels scared and intrigued me, but it had to be done and I had 24 hours to do it. I first went to the Committee where Dr. Siebenschein congratulated me and recommended a nearby room where I left my suitcase and typewriter. Then I visited Susi Kruger. Fortunately she was home in her telephone-booth attic. When I asked for Karla's whereabout, Susi's face brightened.

"Is Ted safe?"

I could truthfully say that he was. I was relieved to hear that Susi knew where Karla now lived: in Mons, a short bus ride from Brussels. I had to hurry, time was getting short. My apprehension increased as the bus approached Mons. How was I to face Karla? I fantasized several scenerios, all upsetting.

I walked slowly to the address Susi had given me. It was a small apartment house with a front yard behind an iron gate, similar to the one where the Bidous lived, my Brussels hosts for one night. I rang the bell and a surly *concièrge* shuffled out and asked   what I wanted. Mademoiselle Berman was gone for the weekend. I was frustrated and relieved. I had booked a flight to London for the next day. For a moment I considered postponing the flight but then took the cowardly way out. I convinced myself it was better so. I asked for paper and envelope, and explained to Karla that I was on my way to England. I enclosed the address Wolf had given me, and wrote an urgent appeal ending with the words: "Ted loves you, he understands, and NEEDS you." I asked her to let me know, and added Max's address in London where I would stay.

The next morning the world was wrapped in a gray mist, matching my mood. The airplane was an eight-seater and I the only passenger. When it lifted into the air, I saw the firm ground sink away from under me — the continent of Europe, Austria, Vienna, my childhood home, Merxplas. Under my seat were my earthly possessions — a suitcase full of clothes and a typewriter. I was in an airship flying through dense grayness into the unknown.

Then the plane broke through the clouds, and above was the fireball of the sun in a clean-scrubbed azure sky.

XI. Three Letters

1.

Whatever else I know about the Merxplas Experiment is contained in three letters and one short report.

In London I lived with Max and his parents in a small flat in Swiss Cottage. They had been able to have some of their Viennese furniture and dishes shipped to their new home, so I lived in familiar surroundings because I had spent many hours in their Vienna home. Max's mother took me in like a son and prepared special meals for me. She was a fabulous cook, and made tasty dishes out of milk, farina, rice and barley. I shared a tiny bedroom with Max — a welcome change from the cavernous dormitory with forty snoring, groaning, coughing men. In Vienna, we had discussed our story ideas walking the streets between our apartments, about 40 minutes apart. In London we talked about our ideas in the bedroom we shared.

But my mind was not on frivolous stories. Most of the time I was writing a book manuscript about Merxplas and reading about the detention camps that were springing up all over Europe. These were different from the death camps being built in Germany and Poland. They were camps for refugees with no place to go. As I look back now, the twentieth century turned out to be the century of refugees — from Vietnam, Central America, Ethiopia, Israel, the Soviet Union. The Hitler refugees were the guinea pigs. In my notes I find lists of camps, now forgotten, where people lived in limbo. Too often it was the next-to-final solution. In Czechoslovakia 2,000 lived in camps near Prague and Brno; in Poland, 2,000 were kept in Posen, Sosnovice, Turnow and Nowosiolki; in Rumania, 500 were housed in camp Carmen Silva; in Switzerland, I,000 were crammed into camps in Nesslau, Albis, Hasenberg, Stäfa, and Basel; in Holland, 3,500 were massed in 26 camps including those of Vesenhuizen, Renver, Hoeck, the quarantine station in Rotterdam, and the Lloyd Hotel in Amsterdam; in France 500 stayed in Martigny (after the outbreak of war there were many more, the most infamous in Drancy), and 140,000 refugees from the Spanish civil war subsisted in Le Barcarès, St. Cyprien, Agde, Bram and Gurs.

During the first few weeks I received letters from my friends in Merxplas — mostly calls for help, and I was so helpless myself. I tried to find a way to get my parents out. The only way to get a British visa (unless one had an American affidavit and one hundred pounds) was for women willing to work as servants, and for husbands who joined their wives as domestic couples. I went to Bloomsbury House where something like a slave market had been established. Londoners looking for maids, cooks, footmen, or chauffeurs came shopping to us who extolled the domestic talents of our relatives and friends. Only people who had a firm contract were given entry visas. No one wanted to employ my parents, who were in their late sixties. I was able to find employment for a second cousin.

My thoughts were still with my former fellow-internees, especially Benedikt and Berman. Although I had written to Benedikt I received no reply, and I worried about his being caught between his loyalty to Natascha, and his attraction to influential Helen. I had, of course, no hope of hearing directly from Berman. I asked Willy Kruger if Susi knew anything about Karla. I received his letter on May 15.

"The camp hasn't changed much since you left," he wrote. "Sommer is gone, he got the same kind of British visa you got, and you may run into him in London if you don't watch out. His fat head is matched by his thin skin. Two men from Pavilion B received visas — one from Panama where he has a brother, the other to Bermuda. Rumors have it that he bribed the De Vries woman, but I don't believe it. She hasn't come up with any visa.

The big news is that Wolf was stripped of his position as chief of police. Vandenheuvel was under pressure to punish him for his unexplained and unauthorized absence from camp just before you left. It seemed not such a big penalty to me, but Wolf is taking it hard altough he puts up his I-don't-care-a-damn front. I guess his gold star meant more to him than anything he achieved in his life. Neidhart has taken his place. He is tough but has trouble with the Wolf gang. Since Heino is no longer The Law he stirs up unrest where he can.

I have my hands full in the sick room. Another doctor has taken Berman's place, an X-ray specialist from Vienna. Although we don't have any X-rays he's a big help. Waniek has become a nurse, taking your place. Kraus is running the canteen.

No new about Berman, but Susi writes that Karla has disappeared. We are hoping that a family camp will be established, so at least Susi and I can be together again.

We miss you, especially your typewriter. Yours, Willy."

No mention of Benedikt.

2.

I finally received a letter from him in August, in response to repeated urgings.

"Please forgive my unforgivable silence," Benedikt wrote. "I've gone through something of a crisis, and so has the camp since Wolf is no longer chief of police. He craves power. Whether he gets it through revolting against law and order or through enforcing it, seems to make no difference to him. Now that he had to turn in his gold star he is the gang leader again. There is a lesson here somewhere.

"Almost all those you sent greetings are still here. We lost our Führer, though. Holländer and his wife left for Buenos Aires. He had pull at the Committee, and the first visa Cecilia Horse-Face has come up with went to him. We hear that our Lilliput tyrant is now dishwasher in a restaurant, and his wife again wears the pants. His presidency of Merxplas is a sweet memory.

"His successor here is *Herr Professor* Klingenberg. He, too, wants to play dictator and he and Wolf are eyeball-to-eyeball. It doesn't bode well for our pocket democracy. That you think of us often I can believe. You helped form our little tribe, at a difficult time — a time, I think, none of us will ever forget. It gave us at least the illusion of a purpose. We were victims and it made us feel masters, at least in a corner of our lives.

"Everything else is the same. Lobositz is still kitchen chef and by his mere presence protects his lame daughter, at least as long as his Nazi friend keeps his word. Schramek still trumpets at mail time, Hutt starts our day with push-ups, Kraus tries to regain some of his 2,000 stolen francs through profits at the cantine, Berliner daydreams of Hollywood, Neumann cheers us with his sketches on Sundays and retrains to be a furrier during the week, Kruger gets his medical practice in our sick room, and Berber wastes his talents as a nurse.

"War seems imminent. What will happen to us then?

"Still, in hope, in spite of everything, Jakob."

No word about himself, Natascha, or Helen.

3.

The third letter came from Franzl Jäger, just before Christmas 1939.

"It's happened." he wrote. "After Austria, the Sudetenland, Czechoslovakia, and Poland, someone finally stood up to punch it out with Hitler. Now the Jews in Poland have become refugees, too, but maybe others will be spared — in France, Belgium, Holland, Switzerland.

"As soon as war broke out, all refugees had to register, and a number of new camps were set up to house them. Many Merxplasians help out in the new camps. I myself am now in a youth camp of Exarde, near Ghent. It has room for 200, and it's a former sanatorium, with no fences, so we can get a pass and just walk to Ghent. The Belgian cops have learned to trust us, I guess we in Merxplas set a good example. They check our passes but nobody wants to escape because we know it's safer to stay in camp than to hack it outside, illegally. Hutt is in charge of Exarde and he's a tough drill sergeant. I'm a sort of boy scout leader, and we sing songs around a fire in the courtyard. Glogau's here, too.

"Another camp was established for married couples, in Marneffe, about 70 kilometers from Brussels, in the Ardennes. You won't believe it, this camp is in a castle in the midst of a huge park. It has room for 480 people, couples and their children up to l6 years. Kruger is there with Susi, as head of the sick house. Georgie Kellner is the bossman. Some married teachers have been transferred to Marneffe, and a school program is being worked out for the kids.

"Merxplas itself has gotten a sister colony, camp Wortel, for the orthodox who are getting koscher food there. It's only five kilometers from Merxplas and under Vandenheuvel. Klingenberg is superrabbi. I hear it's rather primitive, a couple of barracks for about 150 people, but you'd be surprised how many have discovered their orthodoxy because the koscher food is supplied by the synagogue in Antwerp and supposed to be good.

"All these camps follow the model of Merxplas — retraining, language courses, self-government. Merxplas itself has a lot of new inmates because our old friends have been transferred to the new camps. There is no market for retrained carpenters or electricians, but people retrained in running refugee camps are in demand. Well, we have learned *something* useful. Dr. Siebenschein is running Merxplas.

"Wolf and his gang have disappeared. There are rumors that they had something to do with a boat that was captured near Zeebrugge, full of booze smuggled in from Scotland. No one knows where they are, but I'm not worried. They have the most useful profession in this gangster world.

"The best news I saved for last. Koloman Gal left the camp to marry his Lucille and uses what he learned in Merxplas on his father-in-law's farm in Turnhout. Berber got a contract from a dancing outfit in Sao Paulo and left in September. And Benedikt and Natascha got a visa to the Belgian Congo, supposedly through the Pleienbergs. He was very tight-lipped about it. I hear he is trading ivory in Leopoldsville, not exactly the ideal job for an attorney who tried to set up a democracy in a camp for vagrants, but we all would be happy to work anywhere, anything. Uselessness is our greatest curse.

"I've got to run and get ready for an evening of entertainment. All my best,
Franz."

4.

In February I received my American visa and arrived in the United States March 3, 1940. In May the German army overran Belgium. I had ghastly visions of Nazi troups entering Merxplas where the Jewish refugees were offered on a platter, to be shipped to Germany for the "final solution." There was no way of communicating until after the war. In 1945 I wrote to Vandenheuvel at Merxplas and many months later received a note from the Ministry of Justice, saying that all inmates of Belgian detention camps were taken to the French border and released there before Belgium capitulated.

This was good news in only a limited sense. When the German army conquered France, many of my friends might have been caught once more. I have never been able to find a trace of any of them but the memory of Merxplas keeps coming back in my mind like a troubling song.

Benedikt and Natascha were safe, but I will never know whether their escape to the Congo was a gift from Helen Pleienberg, and at what price. I was hoping that Karla's disappearance from Brussels meant that she had joined her husband in Holland, and that they survived the Nazi occupation of that country. I speculated that Wolf and his friends had sought the shelter of Merxplas to await the arrival of their smuggler boat in safety, and that his appointment as "police chief" interfered with their plans in an unexpected way. For the first time in his life he found himself in a situation where he was trusted, and he responded by using his considerable talents to convert his gang into a police force. When he lost his gold star he and his friends became outlaws again. All this was material for stories I never wrote. They survived as fossils in the tar pit of my memory.

My German manuscript about Merxplas was useless in America, and by the time I mastered the English language, I was busy editing scientific papers for the University of California. Only after my retirement and involvement with Dr. Viktor Frankl's existential logotherapy, dreams and recollections of Merxplas forced me to excavate the fossils.

Was the Merxplas Experiment a success?

How can one claim anything a success where most of the participants perished? But it was not an experiment in surviving; it was an experiment in living — in the art of living during the time allotted to us. Is it egocentered rationalism when I see the success in providing one more example of what human beings are capable under the most trying circumstances? Dr. Frankl, in his *Man's Search for Meaning,* writes of inmates in Auschwitz walking into the gas chamber with courage and dignity. In Merxplas, I saw this courage and dignity not in facing death but in trying to build life. But such examples have value only if others know about it. That is why I wanted to write this book.

As for me, the Merxplas experience set the switch for my life. I found role models in Judge Stein who showed me the importance of the search for order in a chaotic world; Benedikt who demonstrated the value of community; Dr. Berman who lived the merits of commitment; Wolf who responded to an unexpected task; Berber who proved the healing power of humor; and many others who accepted the unavoidable and lived within their available limits.

The Merxplas experience also started me off on a search for a world view that answered, at least in part, the questions life asked of me. The Ruler of the Universe was no longer the arbitrary giant who stamped out humans like ants. The Ruler of the

Universe was the creator of a web in which order, community, commitment, response-ability, humor, fate and freedom had their places, and allowed us to spin our own small corner of the web where we are not victims but masters of our lives. Some strands of this web are dark indeed but even they help us feel our connectedness.

XII. Merxplas Revisited

1.

In 1938 I had been forced to go to Merxplas against my will. When I wanted to see the camp 50 years later, it was not so easy to get in. It took a year of correspondence with various officials at the Ministry of Justice, until I received a letter from *Le Directeur Général de l'Établissements Pénitentiaires et de Défense Sociale* telling me that my request was granted but that I personally had to go to Brussels to pick up the permit.

On July 20, 1988, our friends in Düren, West Germany, drove me and my wife to Brussels, only two hours away. At the Ministry of Justice we were met by a pleasant young man who spoke English much better than I spoke French. When I showed him the letter from *Monsieur the Directeur*, the red tape began to unwind. We were passed from room to room, and eventually landed in an anteroom where we were offered coffee, and after a few minutes the Chief of Police entered. He showed extreme understanding for my request and obviously was regretful about what happened in his country to the refugees in 1938.

I half expected him to say *"une formalité"* but he didn't. He gave me a three-line letter authorizing our party to visit Merxplas the next day at 10 a.m.

Our friends drove us through the village of Merxplas (spelled "Merksplas" in Flemish) where most houses were built in the same style of red brick that I remembered so well. We turned into a road with the sign "Strafinrichting Merksplas." There still was no wall or barbed wire separating the camp from the outside. The social experiment was still in progress.

We drove by the hedge which had been the border of our republic. Behind it squatted two warehouse-like buildings, familiar and strange. I recognized them as pavilions A and B. They had been whitewashed, and I discovered the red brick under some peeling paint. Yes, these were the warehouses where we had been stored half a century ago. The soccer field had been replaced by well-trimmed flower beds and there were paved walkways where we had stamped through the mud.

We parked in front of the Administration Building, also whitewashed. It had been off-limits 50 years ago and still was a fortress. We had to show our letter of permission to a guard who studied it carefully and, for the first time, a gate was unlocked. I had never set foot in this building during my stay in 1938. I had only seen Director Vandenheuvel, in his blue uniform and his five-striped cylindrical hat, walk to our pavilions to take inventory or settle disputes.

We were informed that *le directeur* was unavailable but his assistant would give us the guided tour. After a few minutes the assistant director of Merxplas appeared—no uniform, no cylindrical De Gaulle hat, no stripes. She was a woman in her thirties, handsome and feminine, in a white blouse and pink suit, her auburn hair knotted in back. With her was a uniformed man—the main warden. They both spoke flawless English. She took us to a large room where coffee and cookies waited on a large conference table. This was the room, she explained, where monthly decisions were made about the release of inmates. We sat around the table, munching cookies. Neither of them knew much about what happened here in 1938, although the warden's father and grandfather, both dead, had been guards at Merxplas. They gave us some statistics.

The camp still contained vagrants, picked from the streets and slums, 750 at present. The camp had room for more than 5,000 and at times had been full. In 1938 it held about 3,000. The inmates went through retraining classes (had they picked up that idea from us?) such as carpentry, weaving, printing, and farming. They received low wages and when they earned and saved 15,000 francs ($600), inflated from 200 francs in 1938, they were released. The camp contained two additional groups: mentally ill criminals and illegal immigrants. (Perhaps this, too, was an idea for which we had been the guinea pigs.) At present, about 50 illegals were kept at Merxplas. In contrast to our situation, present "refugees" could be held for only one month, then they were either allowed to become legal immigrants or shipped back to their homeland. In 1938, the first would have been life saving, the second a death sentence.

We were given the grand tour. All buildings were whitewashed in antiseptic uniformity. When we entered Pavilion A I felt a leap of anticipatory panic. But there was little I recognized in this silent emptiness except the cement walls, floors, ceilings, and the barred windows. I walked about like in a strange museum, and saw only the unfamiliar—the central heating, the sinks with warm running water, the flush toilets. I peered into the dormitory, forty beds still lined up like piano keys, yet painfully different from my memory. The walls went up to the ceiling, gone were the moralizing sayings, the connecting arches that allowed verbal horseplay with the inmates of the neighboring dorm before light-out time. I tried to remember where my cot had stood, but couldn't be sure. I looked in vain for the various cubbyholes—Waniek's canteen, Holländer's presidential pigeonhole, Berman's telephone-booth examination room. No more iron stoves with uplifted flumes to be stoked with the pages of Aristotle, no more schoolroom desks attached to the seat, no more primitive long troughs to wash up at cold-water faucets. The library had uniformly bound books, some even in English, perhaps left from our collection. I checked. The *Ruler of the Universe* was still there, in French. But also *Huckleberry Finn*, probably the copy I read here 50 years ago. I welcomed the old friend.

I stepped outside on what was once the soccer field and looked toward the steepled church, which had been red brick, and was now whitewashed like the other buildings. There had been Berman's sickroom where I played nurse. I walked toward it and suddenly gagged. A moment later I realized that I stood on the spot where once had been the row of stinkhole toilets. And suddenly I was surrounded by the sounds, the sights, the smells of the past. The flower beds turned into the soccer field again, the bright midday was filled with damp morning fog, and hundreds of hazy figures jumped, clapped, and did push-ups. I walked back to the dorm, dark and filled with shouts, groans, and wails. Ghosts were peering from corners long since built over. Kostelka, his face crinkled with laugh lines no longer used; Judge Stein beavering away at his files with suspects; Wolf, red scarf bulging under his clenched chin; Berber's boyish face hamming it up for a patient. From a bench in the dining room Schramek was barking names at the whirling mob waiting for mail; friend Benedikt spluttering rapid-fire words outlining his ideas; Berliner reminiscing in his Shakespearean voice while a long worm of ash formed on his cigarette and dropped in his lap. In the library our clump of gold-star bearers huddled to make decisions that once seemed monumental, and behind the pavilion the garbage cans were resurrected on which I had placed my portable to write my life-saving trivia. Specters of men flitted by whose names I had forgotten but whose hunched-over despair, utterly confused eyes, and perpetual irritability had kept nagging at me for all these years.

When I think of Merxplas today, I do not see the tidy stillness of the camp in 1988 but the jumble of struggling humans who taught me that life does not always offer happy endings, and that we are not the helpless victims of our fate but its cocreators.

Postscript

The world is full of improbabilities. After the manuscript was completed I spoke to an old friend from Vienna who lived in Los Angeles and mentioned my Merxplas book. She said her cousin in New York was married to a woman whose brother, she believed, had been interned in Merxplas. His name was Mikel Carvin. I remembered no one by that name but wrote him anyway.

An excited answer came back. "Mikel Carvin" was now the name of the young artist whom I had known as Kurt Goldner and whom I named, in my manuscript, Hermi Schaub. Since we had both changed our names drastically, he had escaped my search for Merxplas survivors, and he could not suspect, had he chanced to see my articles or books, that I was his former co-refugee Epstein.

We got together, and the story he told me was even more dramatic than most other odysseys of holocaust survivors.

I had completely forgotten that at our Merxplas Festival in March 1939 Kurt Goldner (alias Hermi Schaub) had not only adorned the walls of Merxplas with his cartoons, but also had a small exhibit of serious drawings. Since I left the camp shortly afterwards I didn't know that a Belgian minister, who had seen the drawings, arranged an interview for Kurt with the director of the Academy of Fine Arts in Antwerp. Kurt received a Royal Scholarship which resulted in his release from Merxplas and intensive instruction at the Academy. He was so gifted that one of his teachers arranged a one-man show for him, to open May 10, 1940. This happened to be day of the Nazi invasion of Belgium. When Kurt arrived at the exhibit, he found the building burning from a bomb hit and watched his paintings go up in flames. He fled the German advance arriving at Dunkirk where he witnessed the evacuation of the English troups but he himself was left behind. He continued his flight to France, was trapped in a bombed building at Calais, and was later dug out by the SS troups freeing the approach to the port area. That's when he assumed the name of Mikel Carvin and, to explain his knowledge of both German and French, pretended to be an Alsatian. The German army used him as an interpreter for war prisoners. When he recuperated enough from his injuries, he took off, returning to Brussels. There he got a job decorating a club restaurant which German officers used as a brothel. He became quite popular among the German officers, and one of them, General von Falkenhorst, commander of the western forces, asked him what he could do for him.

Mikel, who agonized at the thought of his parents living endangered in Vienna, decided to try and save them. He told the general he wanted to attend the Vienna Art Academy and received a pass to travel to Vienna. There he found his parents who had been forced to give up their comfortable apartment and lived in a one-room flat. He stayed with them, was discovered to be Jewish, and had to do forced labor under SS *Sturmbahnführer* Witke, carrying furniture from homes of deported Jews to storage rooms where "Aryans" picked out what they wanted. When Witke learned that Mikel knew something about art and in Antwerp had learned how to restore paintings, he delegated him to scout for valuable paintings from Jewish homes. To permit Mikel to restore these paintings, Witke let him have a large apartment where Mikel could live with his parents.

In November 1941 the systematic shipments of Jews to concentration camps became widespread. Witke, wanting to keep his profitable arrangement, told Mikel that he could protect him from deportation, but not his parents. When Mikel refused, Witke offered to let Mikel's mother stay but his father had to go. Mikel refused again and, with his parents, went underground in Vienna until he found a smuggler who took all three across the border to Yugoslavia. From there they fled to Rumania where, in the fall of 1942, they were arrested and deported to Transnistria, the region between the Dnjester and the Bug where they were interned in a camp in Mobilev. Mikel was ordered to a work battalion to clear minefields. By chance a Rumanian lieutenant was made to believe that Mikel was experienced in leather processing and facilitated Mikel and his parents to be returned to Rumania to a leather factory in Bacau.

It soon became obvious that Mikel had no idea about the preparation and cutting of leather and was demoted to the "stink hole" where the hides were curried. A German commission came regularly to check the quality of the leather produced and was looking for someone speaking German. Once again Mikel's charm won out and they made him foreman of the department producing leather helmet linings. He held that position from Spring 1943 to Spring 1944 when the Russian army approached. His work was satisfactory and his German supervisor never found out about his sabotage: when the approved leather was shipped to Germany, Mikel placed some baby rats into the crates so the leather arrived in Germany all chewed up.

As the German army retreated, Mikel was asked to help dismantle and remove the factory to the south. At this point, he hid his parents and joined the underground in Rumania. When the Russians occupied Rumania in the summer of 1944, Mikel and his parents went to Bucharest. There he met and married Sophie, a Rumanian interior designer. They worked together to furnish the stores reclaimed by returning Rumanian Jews. By the end of 1945 Mikel's parents received an American affidavit from their daughter who had managed to reach the United States before Pearl Harbor. Mikel and his wife went to Vienna to see if any of his family had survived. None had. They went to Paris where they established themselves as interior designers. In 1949 they joined Mikel's parents and sister in New York. Mikel is now a successful interior designer in New York. Among his regular customers are prominent people in the performing arts and professions.

References

1. Consistoire Central Israelite de Belgique. "*150* ans de Judaism en Belge," 1980.
2. Epstein, Josef. "The Refugees in the Vagabond Camp." The Jewish Chronicle, London, February 1939.
3. Fabrizius, Peter. "Im Flüchtlingslager Merxplas." Pariser Tageszeitung, March 22, 1939.
4. Garfinkle, Betty. "Des Belges face à la persecution raciale." L'Institute de Sociologie de l'Université Libre des Bruxelles, 1965.
5. _____. "Belgique, terre d'accueil, problems du refugié." 1938-1940. Brussels, Edition Labor,1974.
6. Grote Winkler Prins Encyclopedie, 1979, p. 255.
7. Schmidt, Ephraim. "Geschiedenis van den Joden in Antwerp."S.M. Ontwikkeling,1963.
8 Steinberg, Maxime. "L'Etoile et le fusil." Brussels, Vie Ouvrier, 1983.
9 Weingarten, Ralph. "Die Hilfeleistung der westlichen Welt bei der Endlösung der deutschen Judenfrage." Bern, Peter Lang.

Appendix

AUFRUF
an alle Flüchtlinge

Die internationale Spannung, die von Heute auf Morgen zur Katastrophe eines Krieges führen kann, veranlasst uns, den von Belgien in so gastfreundlicher Weise aufgenommenen jüdischen Flüchtlingen so eindringlich wie möglich ans Herz zu legen, sich in diesen kritischen Tagen noch mehr als sonst der gewährten Gastfreundschaft würdig zu erweisen.

Noch mehr als sonst wird in dieser Periode allgemeiner Nervosität die Bevölkerung des Landes alles was fremd ist als fremd empfinden, obwohl es nicht zweifelhaft ist, auf welcher Seite die Sympathien des jüdischen Flüchtlings sind. Wenn die friedliebende Bevölkerung Belgiens, die in den Kriegsjahren 1914-1918 Schwerstes erdulden musste, wiederum in einen Krieg hineingerissen werden sollte, muss ein Fremder, trotz aller behördlichen Gegenmassnahmen mit Zwischenfällen jeder Art rechnen.

Es liegt daher im persönlichen Interesse eines JEDEN FLUECHTLINGS bis auf weiteres :

1) auf der Strasse und auf der Tram überhaupt nicht zu sprechen ;

2) das Herumgehen im Zentrum der Stadt zu vermeiden ;

3) das Gebäude des Comités nur in dringenden Fällen zu betreten ;

4) öffentliche Lokale, wie Cafés, Kinos, Restaurants usw. überhaupt nicht aufzusuchen.

Das Comité, das sich für das Wohl aller jüdischen Flüchtlinge, ob unterstütz oder nicht, verantwortlich fühlt, macht aus dem Gefühl dieser Verantwortung heraus diese vier Empfehlungen den Flüchtlingen zur strengen Pflicht, da ihre Nichtbeachtung ernste Folgen nach sich ziehen kann. Wer von den von uns betreuten Flüchtlingen dieser Pflicht zuwiderhandelt, **wird ohne weiteres mit allen sich daraus ergebenden Folgen von unseren Listen gestrichen.**

Es ist von unserer Seite dafür Sorge getragen, dass Uebertretungen sofort zu unsrer Kenntnis gelangen. Ausserdem sollte uns jeder Flüchtling bei der Durchführung dieser Massnahme durch zweckentsprechende Einflussnahme auf eine Umgebung unterstützen.

COMITE D'ASSISTANCE AUX REFUGIES JUIFS,
BRUXELLES.

Call to all refugees from the Jewish Committee in Brussels
•Not to talk at all in streets and in streetcars
•To refrain from walking around in the center of the city
•To enter the building of the Committee only in emergencies
•Not to visit public places such as coffeehouses, movies, and restaurants.

Au Centre des réfugiés de Merxplas

Anvers, 2 décembre.

Un contingent de 74 réfugiés autrichiens est arrivé à la Colonie de bienfaisance de l'Etat à Merxplas.

La population de cette institution est actuellement de 240, parmi lesquels on compte quatorze médecins dont 3 spécialistes, 7 dentistes, et une vingtaine d'avocats, ainsi que de nombreux étudiants. Il y a deux jours, les réfugiés ont reçu la visite d'amis et parents venus de Bruxelles par trois autobus. Parmi les réfugiés se trouve également un littérateur, le Dr Epstein, très connu en Belgique.

Above: Certificate of the author's release from Prison à Forest in Brussels in preparation of his transfer to Merxplas.

Below: News item in *Le Soir*, leading daily in Brussels, that the first refugees had arrived in the camp for vagrants in Merxplas, and the author was among them.

Our World within the Vagrant Camp

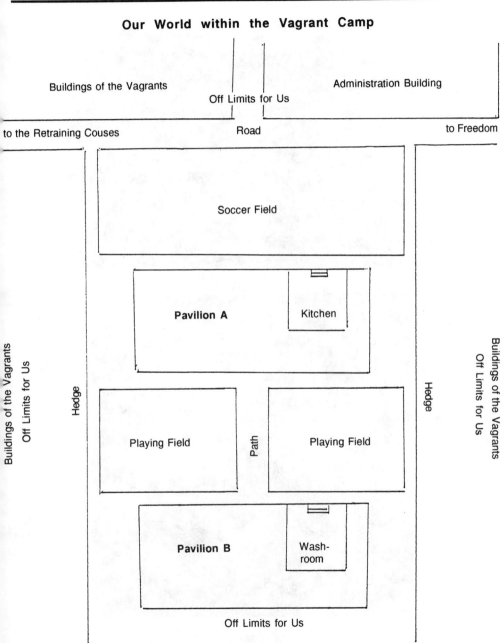

Map of the part of the vagrant camp set aside for the refugees.

Above: Pavilion A in which 160 refugees were housed.
Below: A corner of one of the four dormitories in Pavilion A each of which held beds
         for forty.

Above: Dishing out the food.
Below: Washing dishes.

Above left: The dining hall in Pavilion A where 160 inmates were fed.
Above right: Distributing the mail in the dining hall.
Below: Drying the laundry washed in cold water.

The cartoons on this and the following three pages were drawn by inmate Kurt Goldner (in my book Hermi Schaub), the only other survivor of the camp known to me. See Postscript for details of our rediscovery of each other.

Above: Keeping the floor clean.

Below left: A professor serving food.

Below right: The problem of washing the dishes.

Above left: Self-policing.

Above right: Our self-chosen "King of Merxplas," sitting pretty on the oven stoked by
one of his citizens, offers an extra herring and an apple to another one of his
loyals subjects.

Below: An actual incident. During dish washing one inmate complained of a possibly
broken rib. One of his colleagues, a doctor, examined him, while another, a
lawyer, speculated about damages the injured man may claim.

Above left: Retraining 1. The mysteries of auto mechanics.
Above right: Retraining 2. A student of barbering practicing on one of his fellow inmates.
Below left: Retraining 3. The dangers of plastering.
Below right: Leisure hour.

The real world of retraining:
Above: Would-be farmers march off to work in the morning.
Below: The shoe repair class.

The real world of retraining (continued):
Above: A course for those who are hopeful that blacksmiths
will be needed somewhere in the world.
Below: A student of law switches to auto mechanics.

The real world of retaining (continued):
Above: Metal work.
Below: Poster making.

The program for the Big Event, typed on the author's portable and illustrated by Kurt Goldner (Hermi Schaub). Only three copies existed. One was given to the head of the Jewish Committee, a second to a reporter from *Le Soir*, both lost. The third, shown here, the author kept among his memorabilia.

Pictures from the Grand Opera *Der Goldene Stern (The Golden Star)*.
Above left: The King of Merxplas.
Above right: The Princess from the Committee promising
visas, played by our ballet star Otto Werberg (in the
book named Kurt Berber).
Below: The Grand Finale, a happy ending that remained
wishful thinking: Angels with cornucopias distributing
life-saving visas to illegal immigrants.

This page and the next three pages show some of the serious drawings by Kurt Goldner, based on stories told by inmates who had witnessed such scenes in concentration camps. These drawings were among those that earned Kurt the Royal Scholarship at the Academy of Art in Antwerp.

The author in cartoon and reality.
Above: As inmate in prison (cell 366) and Merxplas.
Below: At Merxplas 1938 (left) and revisiting the camp 50 years later (right) .

Le Commissionné (Délégué)   Bruxelles, le 31.1.1942.
du Chef de la Police de Sécurité
et du Service de la Sûreté pour
le Ressort A I J C N O

II C N° d'Indicateur : 106/42

        Ehc/Po

        Concerne : LE JUDAISME EN BELGIQUE.

                Je vous transmets ci-joint, pour prise de connaissance,
        un rapport sur le Judaïsme en Belgique. Ce rapport fournira, de ma-
        nière concise, un aperçu général sur l'histoire, l'évolution, le
        développement et sur le propre mode de vie du Judaïsme, ainsi que
        sur les mesures prises jusqu'à présent (situation au 31.12.1941)
        contre les Juifs.

                                   (s) EHLERS
                                   Chef d'Elite de brigade d'assaut

*This page and the next two pages contain a document kindly provided by
    Daniel Dratwa, curator of the Pro Museo Judaico in Brussels. It is a report
    to the German Gestapo on the situation of the Jews in Belgium, dated
    January 31, 1942, submitted by the head of the elite of the SS storm
    troops, Herr Ehlers. As Mr. Dratwa recalls, in 1980 in Cologne, Ehlers
    was tried and found guilty of war crimes.*

3/.-

Une comparaison entre le rationnement actuel de la population belge et les quantités mises à la disposition des réfugiés
juifs à l'époque donne le tableau suivant :

	Les réfugiés juifs obtenaient par jour	La population belge obtient actuellement par jour
Pain	250 gr.	225 gr.
Pommes de terre	100 gr.	100 gr.
Viande	75 gr.	35 gr.

De cette comparaison il ressort clairement, sans autres commen-
taires, combien était extraordinairement large l'assistance organisée
du côté juif en faveur de ses réfugiés.

Comme mentionné précédemment, quelques camps de réfugiés
furent créés lors de l'arrivée du flot continu des réfugiés. Avec
le soutien décisif du Gouvernement belge, les 5 camps suivants furent ouverts à partir de 1938 :

Merxplas avec un total de 568 résidents
Wortel   "   "   "   " 184   "
Marneffe "   "   "   " 492   "
Marchin   "   "   "   "   88   "
Exaerde   "   "   "   "   68   "

Le premier de ces camps fut érigé à Merxplas en octobre
1938. Comme il disposait d'un nombre important de grandes salles,
il fut destiné aux hommes seuls âgés entre 20 et 40 ans.

Dans de nombreux cas, des cours de formation professionnelle furent organisés dont la durée fut fixée à 1 an.

Les frais de subsistance dans les camps s'élevaient, par
jour et par personne, à un coût moyen de Frs. 3,78. Le total des
frais d'entretien, comprenant la subsistance, l'habillement, la
formation professionnelle et d'autres frais généraux s'élevait à
un montant de Frs. 7,35 par jour et par personne.

Jusqu'au 31.12.1939, 1156 personnes au total sont passées
par le camp de Merxplas.

Le camp de Marneffe fut mis à disposition par le Gouvernement belge le 1.6.1939. Dans ce camp étaient admises par priorité
les familles nombreuses. Les frais de subsistance s'élevaient à un
montant de Frs. 3,47 par jour et par tête; les dépenses totales se
montaient à Frs. 8,61.

Le camp de Marchin fut érigé en septembre 1939 et était
destiné à recevoir les réfugiés de plus de 45 ans.

Le camp de Wortel fut érigé le 12.9.1939. Ce camp fut agencé
de la même façon que celui de Merxplas. Les dépenses d'entretien dans
ce camp s'élevaient au montant total de Frs. 12,77 par jour et par
personne.   ./.

3;.-

Le camp d'_Exaerde_ entre en activité en novembre 1939.
Il était destiné exclusivement à des jeunes entre 16 et 20 ans.
Il fut projeté de créer dans ce camp une école ainsi que des
possibilités de formation professionnelle.

Une statistique récapitulative de la reconversion professionnelle dans les camps en 1939 est instructive dans la me-
sure où elle montre les centres d'intérêts vers lesquels se tour-
nent les réfugiés dans le choix de leurs situations nouvelles;
les résidents des 5 camps de réfugiés prirent part à la reconversion professionnelles selon l'éventail suivant :

Hommes		Femmes	
Maçons :	22	Coupeuses :	110
Ferblantiers :	13	Tricoteuses :	97
Cordonniers :	50	Chapelières :	49
Ebénistes :	48	Industrie cosmétique :	18
Corroyeurs :	15	Lingères :	52
Electriciens :	39		
Serruriers :	78		
Coupeurs :	58		
Peintres :	48		
Agriculteurs :	174		
Coiffeurs :	6		
Vitriers :	2		

La participation aux cours de langues se fit en 1939
comme suit :

Anglais :   386
Français :   492
Espagnol :   24
Hébreux :   70

En vue de l'entretien de ces camps, les montants suivants
furent dépensés par le Comité bruxellois :

Merxplas :	Frs.	1.265.000
Marchin :	Frs.	42.129
Exaerde :	Frs.	73.589
Marneffe :	Frs.	458.972
Wortel :	Frs.	111.105

Les montants suivants établissent clairement l'importance
du Comité bruxellois au sein du soutien aux réfugiés : L'ensemble
du mouvement des opérations porta en 1939 sur un montant de 17,4
millions de francs. L'année se clôture sur un déficit de Frs. 238.000
Les recettes se composaient comme suit :

American Joint Distribution Committee :	10,9 millions
Total des dons des Juifs bruxellois :	2,7 millions
Hicem :	1,- million
Etat Belge :	1,8 million
	16,4

•/•